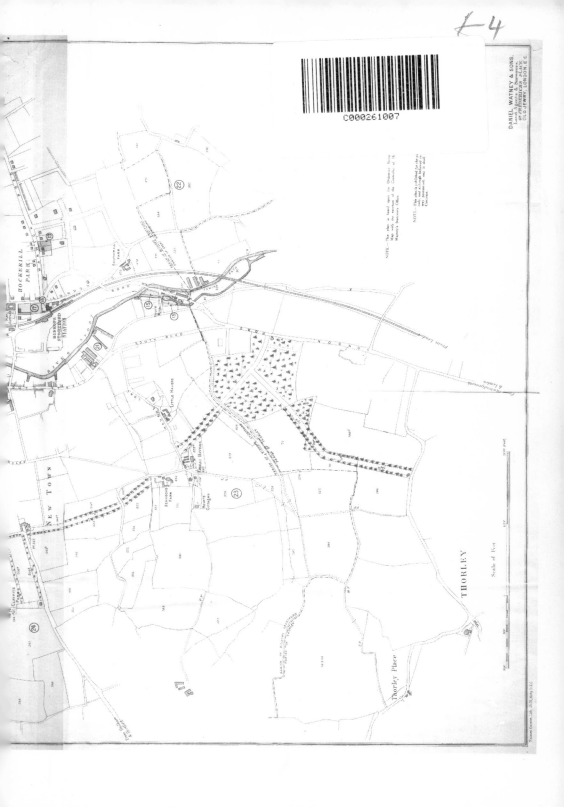

DANIEL WATNEY & SONS,
Land Agents & Surveyors,
44 FREDERICKS PLACE,
OLD JEWRY, LONDON E.C.

L-4

THORLEY

Scale of Feet

Thorley Place

Yesterday's Stortford

FRONT COVER: Crossing the Stort over Station Bridge, c1900.

Bird's eye view of the town at the turn of the century by A. Maxwell, 'Photographer and Picture Framer' of Stortford.

YESTERDAY'S STORTFORD

An album of memories and curiosities

BY

VIOLET SPARROW

BARRACUDA BOOKS LIMITED
BUCKINGHAM, ENGLAND
MCMLXXXI

PUBLISHED IN THIS SECOND (1982) EDITION BY
BARRACUDA BOOKS LIMITED
BUCKINGHAM, ENGLAND
AND PRINTED BY
HOLYWELL PRESS LIMITED
OXFORD, ENGLAND

BOUND BY
GREEN STREET BINDERY
OF OXFORD, ENGLAND

JACKET PRINTED BY
CHENEY & SONS LIMITED
BANBURY, OXON

LITHOGRAPHY BY
BICESTER PHOTO LITHO LIMITED
BICESTER, ENGLAND

TEXT SET IN 11/12 pt BASKERVILLE BY
PERFORMANCE TYPESETTING LIMITED
MILTON KEYNES, ENGLAND

ISBN 0 86023 155 0

CONTENTS

FOREWORD 8

INTRODUCTION 9

YESTERDAY'S TOWN 10

AS OTHERS SEE US 25

MEN OF VISION 38

FAMILIES & FRIENDS 46

MADE BY HAND 71

SONS OF THE SOIL 81

QUEEN'S WEATHER 91

MARKET DAYS 103

NEW TOWN FAIR 121

BIBLIOGRAPHY 137

INDEX 138

SUBSCRIBERS 142

FOREWORD

by Dame Betty Paterson, DBE JP DL

The town of Bishop's Stortford and the surrounding countryside
have seen many changes since the turn of the century. It would
indeed be sad if all knowledge of the colourful characters and old
customs ,which made up the life of the town in the past,
disappeared in the same way as many of the trees and fields
which are now lost to posterity as the town has grown.

In this book Violet Sparrow has, after much research,
produced a most fascinating and diverting background of
incidents and customs, some more respectable than others,
which exist both within and beyond the memory of today's
oldest inhabitants. Future generations may find some of them
hard to believe, but that has made it all so much more
worthwhile to record.

April, 1981

Betty Paterson

INTRODUCTION

This collection of stories and incidents came about through the realisation that we know little about the people who look at us in faded sepia from the pages of our family albums. Notice of intention to write opened up a floodgate of memories.

In 1901, the population of the town was 7,143 and judging by the enthusiastic support I have received, they were all 'characters'. It has not been possible to include everyone; some notable names are missing and others included are as yet unsung.

My thanks to all who showed an interest in the project and who kindly lent their photographs and paintings for reproduction. To Mrs Frost for her collection of J. Kirby photocopies; special thanks are due to Cyril Heath of the *Hertfordshire Mercury,* author of several books, for reading the manuscript and for his encouragement and support; to June Walters for typing the manuscript, Mr Davies of Hertford Museum, Mr and Mrs Wright of Bishop Stortford's local History Society, the Curator of the Rhodes Museum, and the staff of the County Record Office. Thanks are due also to Elizabeth Charvet for her help in research at the Guildhall and to my daughter, Sheila Toomey for her pen and ink illustrations and to my husband, John, for his unfailing help and forbearance.

*Part of a detailed plan of the town centre, 1917, taken from
Watney & Sworder's version of the OS map, 1st Edition.*

10

YESTERDAY'S TOWN

ABOVE: North Street and BELOW: Potter Street from
Maxwell's 'Pictures of Bishop's Stortford'.

AN ACCOUNT OF THE INCOME AND EXPENDITURE

OF THE

NATIONAL SCHOOLS,

AT

BISHOP'S STORTFORD

FOR THE YEARS 1832, 1833, 1834, 1835, 1836, 1837, & 1838,

With Lists of the Subscribers thereto, for each Year.

1832 & 1833.

Dr.

	L.	s.	D.
To Cash, Annual Subscriptions 1832 including arrears	42	10	6
Ditto of Mr. Gee, balance of account in which was included Mr. Houblon's Subscription for 1832, & half a year's rent Dr. Starling due May 1st, 1832.	13	18	6
Ditto half year's rent Dr. Starling, due Nov. 1st. 1832.	13	0	0
Ditto collection after Sermon by the Rev. C. Miller.	12	12	2
Ditto Messrs. Drummond one year's Interest on Turnpike Bond.	2	10	0
Ditto half year's Rent Dr. Starling, due May 1st 1833	13	0	0
Ditto Annual Subscriptions 1833	33	2	6
Balance due to the Treasurer	26	18	6¼
	£157	**12**	**2¼**

Cr.

	L.	s.	D.
By Cash on account of late Master's Salary	2	7	0
Ditto Labourers for work done in School yard	0	14	0
Ditto Mr. David Miller as per bill	5	15	9
Ditto Mr. Bangham ditto	3	16	8
Ditto Mr. Buck ditto	1	15	10½
Ditto Mr. Bear ditto	4	19	3
Ditto Mr. Fordham ditto	4	9	7
Ditto Mrs. Hack ditto	1	3	9
Ditto Mr. W. Wells ditto	0	9	6
Ditto Messrs. Roake and Varty ditto.	4	6	4
Ditto Mr. Perry Insurance 1832 & 1833	1	12	0
Ditto Mr. & Mrs. Vennimore one year's Salary due February 18th, 1833	70	0	0
Ditto Mr. Vennimore (present from the Committee)	5	0	0
Ditto Mr. Jennings as per bill.	1	7	8
Ditto Mrs. Miller, sen. ditto .	9	5	0
Ditto Mr. Cole ditto.	0	5	2
Ditto Bishop of London one years quit rent 1833	0	4	8
Ditto Mr. and Mrs. Vennimore half year's Salary due August 13th, 1833	35	0	0
Ditto on account of quarter's Salary due November 18th, 1833	5	0	0
	£157	**12**	**2¼**

ISAAC DENNING, *Treasurer.*

1833, 1834, & 1835.

Dr.

	L.	s.	D.
To Cash collection after Sermon by the Rev. H. Soames	11	15	2
Ditto half year's rent Dr. Starling due Nov 1st 1833	13	0	0
Ditto one year's ditto Mr. Bear due Sep. 29th. 1833	9	0	0
Ditto donation from Lady C. Phipps, (per Rev. C. Spencer).	5	0	0
Ditto donation Rev. Thomas Pennington 1833 and 1834	10	0	0
Ditto half year's rent Dr. Starling due May 1st. 1834	13	0	0
Ditto Annual Subscriptions 1834	33	8	0
Ditto one year's rent Mr. Bear due Sep. 29th 1834	9	0	0
Ditto half year's rent Dr. Starling due Nov. 1st, 1834	13	0	0
Ditto collection after sermon by Rev. T. Randolph	9	14	6
Ditto Interest on Turnpike bond, Mr. Mott, 1833, and 1834	5	0	0
Ditto Annual Subscriptions	23	15	0
Ditto half year's rent Dr. Starling due May 1st 1835	13	0	0
Ditto one year's rent Mr. Bear due Sep. 29th. 1835	9	0	0
Ditto half year's rent Dr. Starling due Nov.1st, 1835	13	0	0
Balance due to the Treasurer	12	17	2¼
	£203	**10**	**10½**

Cr.

	L.	s.	D.
By Cash Mr. Denning balance due to him	26	18	6¼
Ditto Mr. & Mrs. Vennimore balance of a quarter's Salary due Nov. 18th. 1833	12	10	0
Ditto Labourers for work done in the School yard.	2	3	0
Ditto removing ground under the superintendance of Mr. Tucker	8	8	0
Ditto Mr. Cole as per bill	0	3	0
Ditto Bishop of London two years quit rent 1834 & 1835	0	9	4
Ditto Mr. Perry, jun. for insurance, 1834	0	16	0
Ditto Mr. Emson as per bill	1	6	6
Ditto Mr. & Mrs. Vennimore one years Salary due Nov. 18th. 1834	70	0	0
Ditto Mr. Vennimore (present from the Committee)	5	0	0
Ditto Mr. Palmer as per bill	0	15	0
Ditto Mr. Bradfield ditto	0	6	0
Ditto messenger for distributing notice of Sermons	0	2	0
Ditto the Executors of the late Mr. Peck	4	3	6
Ditto Mr. and Mrs. Vennimore three quarters of a year's Salary due August 18th 1835	52	10	0
Ditto Mr. Vennimore (present from the Committee)	5	0	0
Ditto Mr. & Mrs. Vennimore on account of quarters Salary due Nov. 18th, 1835	13	0	0
	£203	**10**	**10½**

J. H. SUMMERS, *Treasurer.*

Income accounts, National School, 1832-5.

St Michael's School ABOVE: Infants 1921, CENTRE: in class and BELOW: Boys, 1925/6.

13

ABOVE: Herts and Essex High School in its early days and CENTRE: Miss Parsons and her Grimwade House pupils, 1921. BELOW: Bishop's Stortford Hospital, Rye Street.

14

August 15th 1844   At a Meeting of the Trustees
of the Charities of Bishopstortford,
held by adjournment

Present/   Frederick Van Der Meulen Esquire
Mr Joseph Fairman
Mr Joseph Taylor
Mr Renforth Thomas Scarr
Mr John Baynes
Mr Robert Cole

The Churchwardens presented an estimate made
by Mr Cheffins of the Repairs of the Spire of the Church
amounting to the sum of Eighty pounds, together with
his Report which stated that it was getting into decay
for want of such Repairs –

Resolved that this Meeting refer such Estimate and report
to the consideration of the Churchwardens, and recommend
them to carry into effect the recommendation of
Mr Cheffins contained in such Report—

ABOVE: Church warden's accounts in 1844 for repairs to the
spire of BELOW: St Michael's Church.

15

BISHOP STORTFORD,

HERTS.

THREE TENTH SHARES OF AND IN
A CAPITAL FREEHOLD

PROPERTY

TO BE SOLD BY AUCTION BY

G.E.SWORDER

AT THE CHEQUERS INN, BISHOP STORTFORD,
On WEDNESDAY, June 27th, 1866 at Three o'clock,
By direction of the Proprietors with consent of the Mortgagee.

PARTICULARS.
THREE TENTH SHARES

Of and in all that Valuable and very Improvable FREEHOLD ESTATE eligibly situate near Windhill and the centre of the Town. The Premises consist of a large and substantially Timber built and Tiled MESSUAGE now let as 3 Dwelling Houses, containing 6 sitting Rooms, 8 airy Bed Rooms and Closets, 4 Attics, Kitchen, Cellars, and other Domestic Offices; also a MALTING OFFICE which steeps 35 Quarters, with Barley and Malt Stowage for 500 Quarters, and a Brick-built and Slated BAKE OFFICE with 12-bushel Oven, Flour Shop, Sitting Room, and Appurtenances; STABLE and other Outbuildings; 2 Pumps of excellent Water; Extensive and productive GARDENS well adapted for Building purposes; YARD, &c.; also a double COTTAGE or TENEMENT. The whole forming an Area of One Acre, more or less, now let at Rents amounting altogether to £104-2-0 per annum.

The Dwelling Houses, Bake Office, and Gardens are in the occupation of Mrs. Clark and others, and the Malting is in the Tenure of Messrs. Nash; and may be viewed by application to the several tenants.

The entire Property is subject to a Mortgage of £300, also to an annual Land Tax of £3. 3. 6d., and a Quit Rent of 2s. 5d.

Further Particulars may be had at the Office of W. GEE, Esq., Solicitor; and of the AUCTIONEER, Bishop Stortford.

H. COLLINGS & Co., PRINTERS, "OBSERVER" STEAM PRINTING OFFICE, BISHOP STORTFORD.

ABOVE: A substantial property sale in 1866 – with mortgage. OPPOSITE ABOVE: Hockerill Street c1900, CENTRE: South Street c1912 and BELOW: the Cycling Club in the '30s.

16

17

H. COPLEY & CO.'S

ADVERTISER AND RECORD.

1000 COPIES CIRCULATED MONTHLY IN

BISHOP'S STORTFORD AND THE DISTRICT.

| VOL. II—No. 14. | AUGUST 1, 1889. | GRATIS. |

BISHOP'S STORTFORD.

Miss Mary (Minnie) Flinn died at the residence of her father, Mr. Joseph Flinn, on July 8th, at the age of 34 years.

S. B. Findlay (eldest son of Mr. J. A. Findlay, public accountant,) has successfully passed an examination for Chartered Accountants.

The children attending Hockerill Boys' School and Girls' Practising School, had their annual treat in a meadow near the Training College, on July 31st.

The Courts of Foresters have announced their intention of holding their annual fête and gala on the August Bank Holiday. In addition to the usual stage performances by London artistes athletic sports and other attractions will take place.

At the Petty Sessions on July 18th two members of the Salvation Army, Percy King & Henry Murfitt, were convicted of causing an obstruction in South-street; they were each fined £1, and in default were sent to Cambridge gaol for seven days.

At the Herts County Rifle Association's annual Competition at Ashridge, on June 28th, Private Pepper, with 32 points in seven shots at 200 yards, took 1st prize £6, and Lance-Corporal Fletcher 8th prize, £1, with 29 points in the Earl Cowper series; and in the Earl Brownlow series Bugler Nash took £1 with 19 points in five shots at 500 yards.

It has been rumoured more than once during the past month that a new half-penny paper was to be published in Bishop's Stortford, but the reports have so far proved misleading. The cause of its non-appearance has been explained to us, and we are promised that on August the 16th the paper will positively appear.

The Horticultural Society will hold its annual Show at the Grange (by the kind permission of Mr. John Barker) on Aug. 28. The committee have arranged a very attractive programme for the day, including a tennis tournament, balloon ascent, and a grand display of fireworks. Fine weather alone will be sufficient to make this year's show as attractive and successful as any previous one (see advt.).

The Collegiate School, conducted by Messrs. Lockwood and Evans, has during the past week been closed for the summer vacation. The number of pupils of this well-conducted scholastic establishment has been considerably augmented during the present year. On the occasion of "breaking up," the usual prize distribution and entertainment were provided for the boys on Tuesday last.

A rifle match of friendly rivalry took place at the range, Bishop's Stortford, on July 6th, between ten members of the 'L' Company, Queen's Westminster Rifles, and ten of the Haileybury College Company, seven shots each at 200 and 500 yards. At the conclusion of the shooting at 200 yards the boys were only two points behind their more experienced opponents, the scores standing at 281 and 279, but at the finish they were 27 points short, their aggregate being 506 against 533.

Mr. James Blyth, of Blythwood House, Stansted, who possesses some of the finest strains of Jersey stock in the United Kingdom, sent into Bishop's Stortford market on July 4th twenty-two animals for exhibition, being the pick of his herd, including his recent purchases at the Jubilee Show of the R.A.S., at Windsor. Their symmetry of form and clean and healthy appearance was freely commented on, and during their stay in North-street they attracted crowds of spectators. The valuable animals were in charge of Mr. F. Webb (steward), and the stockman, Mr. F. Tucker. Mr. Blyth has since been a successful exhibitor at Horsham and Hatfield, taking several 1st and other prizes.

ABOVE: *H. Copley & Co's* Advertiser and Record *for 1 August 1899 – the town's earliest 'free sheet'. OPPOSITE ABOVE: H. G. Sparrow's postcard of himself – 'the chap with the cap picking hairpins (I said, hairpins) from the lady's head' – and his friends of the Cycling Club at Ye Olde Castle Inn, Cambridge, 1907. CENTRE: Charlie Baker rides to hounds – his greyhounds, exercising in Sworders Field, and BELOW: at the Victory Cup, 3 March 1919, with his trainers.*

East Herts & West Essex News

AND BISHOP STORTFORD ADVERTISER.

No. 306.   SATURDAY, JULY 6, 1895.   One Halfpenny

ABOVE: Cricket Field Lane early this century and BELOW: the Edwardian Hockerill Bowling Club. (The tree is still there.)

By direction of the Executors of the late Sir Walter Gilbey, Bart.

BISHOP'S STORTFORD, HERTS

(And in the Neighbourhood of)

About 32 miles from London, 14 from Hertford, and 25 from Cambridge.

Particulars, Plans and Conditions of Sale

OF THE

FREEHOLD PROPERTIES

COMPRISING

Four Arable and Pasture Farms,

THE RESIDENTIAL PROPERTIES

"ALMA COTTAGE," Station Road,

No. 14, WARWICK Road, Hockerill Park,

The Important Shop and Premises, No. 20, NORTH STREET,

THE BISHOP'S STORTFORD LAUNDRY, Dunmow Road,

The SMITHY in HADHAM ROAD,

VALUABLE BLOCKS OF BUILDING LAND

In Important Positions.

Enclosures of Pasture and Accommodation Land,
Small Holdings, Cottages, &c.,

ALSO AT

STANSTED, ESSEX,

The Residence, Stabling and Grounds,

"SPENCER HOUSE," SILVER STREET,

And a Block of Building Land in Chapel Hill.

To be Sold by Auction by Messrs.

DANIEL WATNEY & SONS

IN CONJUNCTION WITH MESSRS.

G. E. SWORDER & SONS

At the CHEQUERS HOTEL, BISHOP'S STORTFORD,

On TUESDAY, the 27th day of NOVEMBER, 1917,

At TWO o'clock precisely.

Sir Walter Gilbey's estate goes under the hammer in 1917.

Three Maxwell views: ABOVE: the river, CENTRE:
Chantry Gate and BELOW: the Meads.

23

⇒ " The Toreador." ⇐

:: **Characters.** ::

Augustus Traill (of the British Consulate at Villaya) ...	...	Dick Rogers
Pettifer (a Dealer in Wild Animals)	... ...	Bruce Atkinson
Sir Archibald Slackitt, Bart. (Lieut. Welsh Guards) ...	...	Ronald Parry
Rinaldo (a Carlist)	...	Jim Kirby
Carajola (a Toreador)	...	Donovan Cross
Moreno (Carajola's friend)	...	Henry P. Morley
Waiter	...	B. F. Smith
Sammy Gigg (a " Tiger ")	...	Nig Newey
(Note.—" Tiger " was the name given to a groom attending a dog-cart).		
The Governor of Villaya	...	John Brewitt
Bandmaster	...	Alec Ogilvie
Dora Selby (a Ward in Chancery)	...	Muriel Dupere
Nancy Staunton (Dora's friend)	...	Winifred Mason
Susan (Proprietress of the Magazin des Fleurs, Grand Hotel, Biarritz)		Jean Atkinson
Mrs. Malton Hoppings (a Widow)	...	Birdie Orsman
Dona Teresa	...	Vera Buchmannhoff
Cora Bellamy (a Bridesmaid)	...	Betty Furze
Isabella	...	Irene Amey

Chorus of Flower Girls, Visitors, Bridesmaids, Townspeople, Soldiers, etc. :—

Ladies :—I. Amey, M. Andrews, Joan Atkinson, F. Breeze, M Dennis, K. Dennis, M. Devey, V. Fincham, E. Goodman, M. Henderson, K. Ives, B. Lambert, W. Long, D. McDonagh, V. Parry, P. Pegrum, K. Reynolds, E. Smith, G. Smith, I. Walters, V. Wilkinson.

Gentlemen :—J. Brewitt, H. A. Buttery, W. E. Buttery, D. L. Clarke, B. King, J. A. Ogilvie, P. G. Salmon, B. F. Smith, H. Wacey, H. J. Walters, E. M. Zelley.

BELOW: The Toreador was the 1934 Amateur Operatic Society's offering, with ABOVE: Nig Newey and Vera Buchmannhoff.

24

AS OTHERS SEE US

Bishop's Stortford is anciently described as being half marsh and half meadow, and the Causeway was the reputed site of St Osyth's Well, a place of healing for the blind. The diarist Evelyn described the town as a 'pretty watered place with a fussy busyness about the market and a Flemish look to the town'.

'Poor Robin Winstanley', the brother of Henry Winstanley, the architect and builder of the first lighthouse on Eddystone Rock, was 'perambulating' in 1667 from Littlebury to London. He stayed at The Crown Inn (1601–1872) and was so taken with the fine Rhenish and French wines, the Spanish Sack, the powdered beef and pullet that he glanced at the town centre, noted the signs of 'Rams and Horned Beasts', The George and The Reindeer 'where bringing the merry chink, you may have a merry drink'. He advised those interested in the stocks and the cage, which stood at The George corner and later in lower North Street for 200 years, to consult those who had been in them. The stocks and the ducking stool were in The Causeway up to 1745. 'Poor Robin' hurried back to The Crown to pursue the pleasant pastime of 'drinking and tobacco intermixt' for the rest of his stay. Daniel Defoe was another satisfied customer of The Crown.

One local myth persists – that John Denley was burned at the stake (1555) in The Causeway on Goosemead, otherwise called 'God's Meat Green'. In fact he was executed at Uxbridge.

Thomas Pound, whose privilege it was to produce masques for Queen Elizabeth I, instead of being knighted upon completing a difficult dance, was ordered to repeat the performance, slipped and fell, whereupon the Queen tapped his shoulder with her toe and said 'Arise, Sir Ox'. Thereafter he was ostracised by the Court, a blow from which he never recovered. He became a recusant in one of the many prisons he occupied. He is described as a dangerous man given to challenging ministers to dispute, thereby enraging Bishop Aylmer and consequently he was transferred from the Marshalsea Prison to Bishop's Stortford;

described by 'Popish' writers 'this was an obscure, melancholy place void of light and converse'. The castle dungeon is thought to be the convicts' prison mentioned in Strypes' *Life of Bishop Aylmer*. After the Restoration, it was partly demolished. Part 'fell down in the night which frightened the generality the more because one Sedgwick, an enthusiast, had prophesised the end of the world to be that very night'.

An inn was built on the site of the castle prison and was called The Cherry Tree (1649–1840), after the cherry orchard which grew upon the mound. It survived successive floodings, was partly rebuilt with a pretty gabled facade and practically fell apart in the 1930s. It had been the home of Taylors, the maltsters, in the 1900s, then the Gabbs and afterwards the Harmes family. Soldiers were billeted there during the 1914 war, when it was almost obscured by a beautiful magnolia tree. Human remains were found on the north side of the mound and by the moat. The Harmes girls, Muriel and Gladys once played with skulls found in the garden. These were blessed and reinterred by Rev W. McCarthy and forgotten.

Other notable visitors to the town were John Wesley and Rev John Reynolds who were more concerned with the souls of the people than the town's picturesque ambience. John Wesley arrived at the end of the 18th century, a Methodist community was formed in 1823 and the first service held openly was in The Causeway. In 1825, a seed warehouse was converted into a chapel in Church Street.

Exchanging pulpits (1772) with John Angus (1748–1801) Rev John Reynolds, a founder of the London Missionary Society records in his diary his pity for his friends (thought to be the Hawkes family) and prays 'may God keep them from catching the worldly and censorious spirit which reigns in Bishop's Stortford'.

During the depression, the Jarrow marchers visited the town, some finding a night's bed and breakfast at the old Infirmary. In the '20s and '30s, many itinerants on the same mission stopped at the Monastery kitchen hatch for a bite and a cup of tea or visited 'the wayfarer's rest' set up by All Saints' ladies to cater for tramps waiting to enter Haymeads, open to them by 6 pm. This tea stall was in Benjamin Fincham's old forge, near the Georgian house in Hockerill Street. Describing the scene in 1937, Alice Sparrow tells how she and old Mrs Hugh Elliott coped with 12 'gentlemen of the road' mostly from Lancashire.

Afterwards, the tramps chopped logs and gardened in return for a night's lodging at Haymeads.

Part of the duties of porter and ambulance driver Jim Holland was to sell and deliver the logs; the ambulance horse knew the regular ports of call and one such was The Nag's Head on the corner of Haymeads Lane. The old Nag's Head was previously a farm, then an ale house and was demolished in June 1934 when the new Nag's Head was opened behind it. Corn had been stored between the rafters, a usual form of insulation in old farmhouses, against the bitter winters of long ago. Leslie Larman remembers

his father saying how the men arriving on the 6 am train from Barkers of Kensington to work on the extraction of old timbers from Plaw Hatch for Sir Walter Gilbey, prior to his removal to Elsenham Hall in 1875, would call in at The Nag's Head mid-morning for two pennyworth of rum in milk, returning to London on the evening train. The old farm land around The Nag's Head became the scene of circuses and sporting events and Revivalist Meetings. There are memories of the hot tent, lit by oil lamps (1918–1920) when a large canvas bath was sunk in the ground for easy Baptism by immersion, to the repetitive singing of 'Wash me in the blood of the lamb, and I shall be whiter than snow'.

27

It is hard to imagine the fox being run to earth behind a pile of domestic logs in the garden of The Nook, Sandle Road in the '30s. The brush was presented to a former lady of the house, yet it was commonplace in the '20s and '30s to meet Capt Jack Pawle's Beagles being exercised in the country lanes around the town. Capt Pawle and Harry Cox, farmer at Great Havers, were featured with other characters in a painting titled 'The Bench Sits' by John Kinnersley Kirby, RA, who painted other lively local scenes, including the 'Calf Buyer' recently resold in London.

A portrait of Jimmy Sell, freelance journalist, with inky fingernails and that hallmark of Kirby paintings, a flower in his buttonhole, was painted against the background of smokeladen Victorian wallpaper in a 17th century pub, The Star in Bridge Street, and titled 'The Slate Club Secretary'. The work of John Kirby was exhibited in major salons in Paris and New York. He lived in Blythewood Lodge and latterly at Grove Hill, now Kirby Cottage in Stansted. Another of his paintings to achieve nationwide publicity was 'The Ration' featured on a war-time calendar by Raphael Tuck, showing Mr Woodford, the butcher (senior) with a massive cleaver and small chop.

North Street and the Chequers were to achieve fame when a portrait of 'The Landlord of The Chequers' by John Kinnersley Kirby was hung in the Academy. It presented Mr Brazier on the steps of the Hotel with his little black dog. Joe Brazier had a 'Brazier room' developed, with souvenirs of his colourful life and of course the portrait, for which he charged admission.

In 1973, May Alice (nee Hart) and her husband, Bertie Whiffin retired from The Royal Oak. As a young girl, during a period of ill health, May Alice had shown talent as an artist. She drew likenesses of famous people, asking them to autograph her pictures, of which she has a special collection. Another 'special' was sketched in response to an invitation from Joe Brazier to the town's children. A gold watch was to be given as a prize for the best pencil copy of the famous portrait 'The Landlord of The Chequers'. May Alice entered her sketch in 1931 and won the gold watch, which she still treasures.

Arthritis and the war ended John Kirby's artistic achievements; with dwindling strength and memories of the farmers' Thursday luncheons at The Chequers to sustain him, the availability of convenience food was too much for him. 'Whoever heard of fish having fingers?' he would ask.

ABOVE: The Causeway, c1905. LEFT: Grace Calvert Holland of Plantation House who painted The Old Nag's Head. RIGHT: Castle Cottage – The Cherry Tree Inn.

ABOVE: Mrs. Holland's painting of the old farmhouse, once an ale house, The Old Nag's Head, demolished in the '30s to make way for the new Nag's Head; c1890. BELOW: Bridge Street in 1871 by E. Edwards.

ABOVE: Edward's Hockerill (1871). CENTRE: Matron Mrs Friend, Dr Dockray, Matron's daughter (later Dame Phyllis Friend DBE) and Haymeads staff (ambulanceman Jim Holland on right) earlier this century. BELOW: Pearce House, formerly Plaw Hatch, Sir Walter Gilbey's home before he moved to Elsenham Hall.

31

ABOVE: John Kinnersley Kirby RA's The Calf Buyer *with Joe Brazier far left, Mr Humphries (striped suit), Harry Cox (behind him), Mr Routledge (smoking a pipe), Mr Rolfe (behind lad) and Mr Piper (auctioneer). BELOW: Kirby's* The Bench Sits *with Capt Pawle (4th from right) whispering to Harry Cox, Mr Fassnidge (scribe), William Gee (Clerk of the Court) and Chairman Frank Flynn.*

"THE WEEK'S RATION"   *From the Original by J. K. KIRBY, exhibited at the Royal Academy.*

When we queue for our chop in the Butcher's Shop
Our thoughts turn to days of old,
With their choice of Chump or juicy Rump
Of saddle or Sirloin bold.
But as our JOINT efforts are helping the war
In no uncertain fashion,
The CUT's worth while, so with WINNING smile
We take our weekly ration.

C. J. Woodford, butcher of Dane Street in Kirby's Royal Academy picture which Raphael Tuck featured on a World War II calendar.

Kirby's famous The Landlord of the Chequers – *Joe Brazier.*

The Squire of Clavering; *Percy Rolfe as Kirby painted him – his moat was dug up in connection with the infamous Moat Farm murder.*

ABOVE: Kirby brings to life The Kitchen at the George in 1932. *BELOW: W. Basil Worsfold MA compiled a limited edition of signed and numbered copies for subscribers,* Twenty Centuries of England Being the Annals of Bishop's Stortford. *In the prospectus he included his* The Canalized Stort, with Maltings (*drawn 27 August 1931*).

LEFT: Henry Moore, of Perry Green, a familiar Stortford figure for forty years and the world's finest contemporary sculptor. RIGHT: Joe Brazier, sketched in 1916. BELOW: Stortfordians biked and drove to Clavering to view the site of the Moat Farm murder.

LEFT: The Stort at Southmill showing the back view of Duck's Row 1912; RIGHT: Dr Rhodes. CENTRE: Manor of Piggotts and BELOW: Thomas Ashwell and son Percy on his pony Tottie in Lordship Farmyard, Much Hadham, 1887.

MEN OF VISION

Thomas Adderley (1707–1774), landlord of The Crown, was the prime mover in getting the Stort Navigation to the Thames under way. It was to take 11 years to fund the project, get the necessary bill through Parliament (1765) and complete the work on 15 locks in 1769. The grand opening of the Stort canal was an eventful occasion. Hopes were expressed by the chief engineer that Stortford would 'now be open to the ports of the world'. A feast was laid on in North Street, described in George Jackson's diary with humour and restraint: 'The table in the booth was scarce well covered, and the company sat down before the crowd broke in and took all the meat away. It became a scramble after that. It was with great exertion that I saved the wine. When this was a little appeased the bread was cut in lumps and given to the people and after this the ale, being hogsheads, was filled into two large tubs and carried into the streets, where the people might drink that could. Some getting drunk soon, and giving room to fear a riot, and one of the tubs, when full being thrown over, desisted from serving the rest.' However 'the whole confusion was ended without the smallest accident or quarrel that I have heard of.'

By 1800 the benefits were seen to be manifold as the long flat, capacious Stort barges, drawing 2–2½ ft of water, carried vast quantities of grain and malt to the Thames. Coal was carried the other way. Malt dust, pigeon dung and other manures were also disposed of in this manner. A plan to link up with the Cam, although it had powerful support from George Jackson MP, was obstructed by the landowners. It had obvious advantages as grain was being carried from East Anglian ports to London, then down the Lee and Stort to be made into malt in Bishop's Stortford. The advent of the railway, running beside the Stort for most of its navigable course, put the Stort Navigation out of business and made the coaching trade redundant.

An early protege of George Jackson was to become Captain Cook, who named Port Jackson in New Zealand after his patron.

George Jackson took his wife's family name for family and financial reasons and later became Sir George Duckett, Baronet. It is as George Jackson that he is remembered in Bishop's Stortford, where the new shopping precinct has been named after him.

The malting industry was to decline owing to the centralisation of the industry in Lincolnshire. The Corn Exchange became a venue for the Cage Bird Society and other users and was a Synagogue for the Jewish evacuees from the East End during World War II. We were to lose three breweries–Baileys on Dunmow Road, Hawkes and Benskins. The number of public houses steadily declined due to social change. The wine bars are now opening up and we drink more socially, and the vineyards are coming back, one at Purleigh, Duddenhoe End and Cricks Green in Essex. The attitude to temperance in the 19th century and its extremes must be seen against the deprivations of the times. The Ashwell family of Warren Farm, Much Hadham, came from Eaton Bray near Dunstable over 100 years ago, great grandfather Ashwell moving an entire farm and family of 12 children by road to Stortford Park Farm. They were to branch out to the Lordship, Much Hadham and to Piggotts Farm in 1890. The last venture proved a disaster. Crops failed after three successive wet years and Piggotts was vacated.

As a whole the Ashwells were not opposed to ale drinking as a necessary part of the labourer's nutriment, when supplied free by the farmer. From haymaking time to harvest, Percy Ashwell and his brother, when they were boys on The Lordship Farm, Great Hadham, took stone gallons of small beer, five times a day, six days a week to the men working in the fields. They were not expected to work so hard without proper nourishment, but when the men squandered their hard earned pay in ale houses in Bishop's Stortford, the Ashwell family did approve of and supported the temperance movement.

The maltings and the breweries created much employment in their day and the anger of the men employed by Benskins Brewery against the Temperance Movement is understandable.

Joseph Crisp was the target of their anger. They tarred the windows of his drapery shop in Market Street, Bishop's Stortford and they renamed him 'Jesus' Crisp. He was a man of principle and a supporter of temperance. When the local Board met to discuss whether the paupers in Haymeads should be allowed a ration of ale, as was customary at Christmas, it was expected that Joseph Crisp would vote against it, even though his might be the only dissenting voice.

He was also opposed to games of chance. As a member of the Congregational Tennis Club, he was invited to take part in a game, but when with gentle humour it was explained by a friend that there was an element of chance in it, as he would have to *draw* for his partner, 'Jesus' Joseph Crisp declined and withdrew from the game.

Latterly, Joseph Crisp lived in Bells Hill, with his daughter, who was known to declare that she would rather die than let

alcohol pass her lips. She admitted to being more broadminded than her mother, who would not have allowed a hot cross bun in the house.

Another temperance supporter, Joseph Dorrington Day used a picture of a serpent curled up in a wine glass to illustrate the evils of drink to children.

The Temperance Movement was also strong within the Church of England which was deeply committed to eradicating the three and five pot men (1 pot = 1 quart), so popular in the mid 19th century. Mr G. Avery Rolf, lecturing Hockerill College students at the turn of the last century, said that alcohol should be taken only on prescription and administered by a doctor. Mr Rolf warned of the effects on elementary school children of intemperate parents.

Another staunch believer in temperance was Alfred Slaps Barrett who lived in Chantry Road. He enraged the townspeople by giving a consignment of flour he received at his grocery shop, Holland and Barrett (now Budgens) to the German PoW Camp at Oak Hall during the 1914 War, no doubt with good reason. It is not clear whether it was a gift or a business transaction. The people plastered his shop window with hostile slogans. Further, he was alleged to hold the pawn-broker's licence so as to prevent one opening in the town. All was forgiven and forgotten on pleasant Sunday afternoons in the disused chapel which formerly stood on the site of the old cinema. The PSAs were extremely popular and confined to the male population; semi-religious gatherings which gave men something to do on a Sunday afternoon. Most popular of all were the Temperance charabanc outings to Walton and Clacton, which practically emptied the town, though people were sceptical about the rosy complexions acquired after a day at the sea.

Alfred's son Ted reorganised the Town Band in 1928, and designed a new navy-blue uniform with broad light blue chest panel edged with silver buttons. It was not long before a picture of this Band appeared on a box of matches produced at Bishop's Stortford Match Factory. Ted lived in Hockerill Street and created a labyrinth of mixed residential, commercial and light industrial uses in the old maltings and houses behind the Bowling Club. He was an inventive man and created an automatic bellows for his open fire, which blew it out and most of the ash onto the pelmets. His musical talents inclined him to practise the trombone in bed. He published *Tin Can,* a paper aimed critically at the Council. His sister Elsie became first woman Chairman of the UDC. Her name is linked with the club for the blind. Una, liberal in politics, supported social studies for women and the Townswomen's Guild Movement.

Eva, the most colourful of three sisters, became a Court photographer in Rome. Her studio in the Via Margutta was as near an English country cottage as she could manage, with a warming pan from Pipers, a Bishop's Stortford antique shop, chintz curtains and chesterfield, and an open fire which suffered from a damp, unswept chimney. Her wealthy clients were regaled with Christmas pudding and English trifle and Christmas gifts from Woolworths, Bishop's Stortford. Eva designed her own dresses. A mixture of Roman Goddess and the homespun daughter of Alfred Slaps Barrett, clad in white or blue velvet toga and golden hair net, she could be seen at large in Rome in all weathers. The clothes, intended to hide the less attractive features of her outline, drew maximum attention.

Her photography was hand-tinted and much in vogue in Rome in the 1930s; indeed her Christmas tree in 1934 was not hung with baubles but presents from her clients, with a brooch from The Dowager Queen of Greece, pearls from Japan and cameos and corals set in gold. She was the first woman to photograph Mussolini.

Dr W.F.R. Rhodes came to Bishop's Stortford in 1849 renowned as 'the good Mr Rhodes' in Brentwood, where he built a small church at his own expense. He was to divide St Michael's Parish into three and see the building of two further fine churches in the town, before resigning his living after 27 years in December 1876, in his own words 'compelled by infirmity and old age', and perhaps kindly encouraged by the church wardens. There was widespread dismay in the parish and the hope was expressed by the *Herts & Essex Observor* that he would reconsider the matter. A local belief that the church wardens quarrelled with Dr Rhodes persists to this day. St Michael's vestry minutes give no hint of such a disagreement. It is believed that the church wardens' supposed treatment of his father led Cecil Rhodes to leave Bishop's Stortford out of his will. Cecil Rhodes left his half-sister out of the same will and abandoned grandiose schemes for reclaiming America for the Crown.

As a boy Rhodes was a dreamer and spent many idle hours in the garden of South Road, where he was born. He certainly fulfilled the dreams and aspirations of many a Rhodes Scholar—surely an inspired bequest. A sickly boy, pigeon-toed and lefthanded, he attended a Sunday Bible class run by his mother, with a brother and little Miss Barnard, whose father, William Barnard, is recorded in the Bishop's Stortford *Almanac* of 1874 as being a tailor and woollen-draper in the Market Square. She was to tell her daughter, Mrs Claison of Harpenden, how Cecil passed the home of a retired Admiral on his way to school daily and was puzzled to see the old gentleman planting trees. 'But you won't live to see them fine and big', he said. 'No', replied the Admiral 'but others will enjoy their shade for a long long time to come'.

Dr Rhodes was also a tree planter. Having moved into the house in South Road to enable the vicarage to be used in conjunction with the newly reformed Grammar School, he set about refurbishing the garden. The 19th century building boom brought an increasing demand for trees and shrubs of every kind. In 1851, Joseph Tucker had nurseries on the site of the Apton Road Car Park and across the road on the land where the Salvation Army Citadel now stands. He supplied houses and vicarages, farms and gentlemen with a variety of filberts, pines, yews and laurels and arbutus. Between 1851 and 1854, Dr Rhodes bought 12 horsechestnuts, seven laurels, eight filberts, two large yew trees, 30 gooseberry bushes, 30 currant bushes and sundry double furze, rose bushes and a honeycerte at a total cost of £2 4s 4d.

Cecil Rhodes was to become a tree planter himself. The fine avenues of trees which he planted in new settlements proffer comfort and shade in the heat of Bulawayo, Salisbury and Umtali. William Barnard's grand-daughter was to enjoy the shade of these trees herself when she and her husband went out to Rhodesia in 1929, to farm in Umtali for many years.

Cecil Rhodes was also to export garden birds from Bishop's Stortford to Rhodesia but it is not known whether they survived. His mother is buried with two brothers in a grave now incorporated into the garden of a house in Apton Road.

The arrival at Rhodes' birthplace of twenty-five African Chiefs on 1 July 1964, after a fact-finding tour of Pakistan, Northern Italy and Scotland, was a noteworthy occasion. It was memorable if only because of the views expressed by the Chiefs. Those who could speak English were loud in their praise of Rhodes Museum and declared that there was no such collection in the then Rhodesia. Upon seeing the scarlet and plumes of Cecil Rhodes, 'What is this? our Rhodes was a man of peace, he taught us not to war with one another', they protested. But, most surprising of all was the statement that coming to Bishop's Stortford 'was like coming home'.

They were amused at illustrations of their forbears in the early days of Rhodesia. The Chiefs themselves were dressed in black jackets and pin-stripes. They enjoyed English afternoon tea, a far cry from the fare they would have been served in Africa in Rhodes' day. An official of the party from Rhodesia House said that the Chiefs were relatively unimportant people. The Queen, however, honoured Chief Sidola by awarding him the MBE.

ABOVE: Alfred Slaps Barrett's funeral, Congregational Church, where CENTRE: the foundation stones were laid 15 July 1914 for the Sunday School. BELOW: His son Ted (centre front) and the Town Band – a picture used on a locally manufactured matchbox.

ABOVE: An oil painting of Bell's Hill and BELOW: a charcoal drawing of Windhill Lodge by Minnie Roy (Later Mrs Harry Cox); sold for £3000, it opened as St Mary's Convent school for girls, 1896.

FAMILIES & FRIENDS

When the Aldermen of the City of London agreed to let rooms in the Aldgate to Chaucer in 1374, it was also agreed that he would vacate should the gate be necessary for defence against the hordes from the East. It is unlikely they were thinking of commuters from Brentwood or Southend, or stretching a point of the compass, members of the Ticket-holder's Association from Bishop's Stortford. The 'wild men of Essex' were those involved in the Wat Tyler rebellion. Chaucer gave up his tenancy in 1381 about the time that Dick Whittington was to bring fame to the City, honour to himself and a little glamour to us as 'Lord of the Manor of Thorley'. There is no evidence that Dick ever came to Thorley, but as an administrator or trustee he did assume Lordships occasionally. Alice Maria Whittington (1852–1932) was said to be his colateral descendant. She spent the last 40 years of her life in Sawbridgeworth and Bishop's Stortford and was a frequent visitor to Canon Proctor of Thorley. Together they spent summer afternoons boating on the Stort. She was reared by her godfather and uncle, Bishop Claughton, first Bishop of the new diocese of St Albans (1887–90). Upon his death in 1892 she eventually came to reside on Windhill at Norman House and later Elmhurst Lodge, when she was known locally as 'Miss Dick', a daughter of Rev T.T. Whittington, aunt of Canon Whittington of Wakefield and a cousin of Lord Daresbury. She presented a stern Victorian aspect. In some respects she resembled Dick Whittington in outlook without the romantic trimmings of pantomime cat which first appeared in the 18th century.

Miss 'Dick' expressed her disapproval of the Convent girls for laughing loudly in the street. 'Are you ALLOWED to laugh and frolic?' she asked. 'Yes, and sometimes we are allowed to speak' came the impish reply. Miss Dick was known to draw her skirts about her, veering into the road as she drew level with St Joseph's Church, on her way to morning service at St Michael's.

One of her 'good works' was to manage the parish magazine, printed at Mardon's in North Street. She expected them to be ready on Mondays for, she would tell Miss Beeson 'I can't come on Tuesdays or Wednesdays and NEVER on Thursdays because of the cows'.

Miss Dick was said to receive an annual visit from a City of London official; there is no record available, though a visitor came once and finding her out, left his card 'with the corner turned down' at the Vicarage. She had a close and enduring relationship with Lady Phené Neal of Vyse Court, Windhill. When Sir William Phené Neal became Lord Mayor of London, Miss Dick was invited in her 78th year to the Lord Mayor's Show and Banquet in November 1930.

Miss Dick is described as a small slight old lady wearing the usual black, and a bonnet with long ribbons. The boys in St Michael's Sunday School tied the ribbons to the leg of her table and when she stood up, off came the bonnet to reveal a nearly bald head. It was then that Rev William McCarthy persuaded her that it was time to retire.

She befriended Miss Molly Eaton, known as 'Pussy Eaton', either because of her association with Miss Dick or the cat she carried on her shoulders. Her family was said to have given their name to Eaton Square. She was living in reduced circumstances. Her father was once chaplain to the Infirmary and she had a small income, augmented by the proceeds from the sale of fine clothes sent to her periodically by a Church organisation. Miss Eaton also gave piano lessons at sixpence per hour and sought to pay her way with amateur water-colours of Windhill. Hers was a childlike simplicity. She walked jauntily around the town, swinging a Dorothy bag behind her; having no means of support, her stockings sagged to her ankles, a plight to which she was airily indifferent. One day on a sketching outing in Basbow Lane in the '20s, a rundown area in those days, Alice Maria Whittington was heard to say 'It's no good, my dear, we can't live together if we can't tell each other the truth'.

Another Victorian character was Billy Peck (1845–1921). He showed humorous indifference to social customs but, when expedient, he could exploit them with style. He left home in Hoxton aged 14 years and came to Bishop's Stortford as a young man and married a young sea captain's widow, Sarah Anne Swann-Powell (1846–1944), a woman of refined taste who ran a fish shop in South Street. William Peck was a fish wholesaler and the fish business grew and prospered from this liaision. An entrepreneur and middleman, Billy bought potatoes off the land which were delivered to Bishop's Stortford Station, where they were relabelled and despatched to Covent Garden and other London markets, thus saving on warehousing.

Before catching the 5 am train to Yarmouth to negotiate fish for Billingsgate and his own wholesale business in Bishop's Stortford, he would take down the bugle which hung in his wife's fish shop and blow a reveille up New Path by Holy Trinity Church, to awaken his man, Billy Porter, reputedly deaf and dumb, though Billy Peck actually taught him to speak. Mrs Porter, tired of the dawn serenade, emptied the slops over Billy Peck, to the general satisfaction of neighbours.

Billy did his book-keeping in his astute head or on the walls of his shop. His Yarmouth bloaters and kippers, home-cured, were the talk of the town. On Saturday mornings, sitting on an upturned bushel measure, he greeted his customers and it was said that his voice could carry the names of those who owed him money, as far as Newey's Laundry on Dunmow Road.

Sir Walter Gilbey (1831–1914) congratulated him upon being a self-made man like himself, and a friendship developed between them. When Sir Walter wished to give him a present, Billy asked for a curly brimmed grey bowler like Sir Walter's own, so an order was placed in London with Sir Walter's hosier and hatter. When the bowler arrived, Billy got out his pony and tub and drove round the town to show it off. Corner boys on New Town Road tried to dislodge it with pungent ammunition provided by the pony. The bowler was one of many gifts from Sir Walter and the family treasures a brass tray signed by the baronet and dated 1897. That year, Billy Peck built a house on Gilbey land, No 13 Warwick Road. His interest in the Bishop's Stortford Flower Show, a near professional effort in those days, was not disinterested. After the Show, he wined and dined the head-gardeners of the area on his lawn and cornered the market in fruit netting; his sideboard groaned with out of season fruit and he had the pick of asparagus beds for miles around.

When his rate bill came in, Billy Peck protested to the Council. He now owned much of the property facing Station Road as far as the Stort. At his behest his wife, Sarah Anne confined unpleasant correspondence to the fire. When the rate summons arrived he strode into court and emptied a half pint shrimp measure full of gold coins on the bench with a flourish.

Sir Edmund Barnard, magistrate (1905–1930), said that if he lived in Warwick Road, he would have to pay Warwick Road rates.

Sarah Anne and her daughter Margaret (Maggie) Peck, a pupil at the new Convent School (1897) went on a shopping spree in early Edwardian days, riding outside on a horse-drawn 'bus. Billy made himself at home, taking off his shoes and socks and hanging his feet over the side of the 'bus to cool them, a practice of which the ladies disapproved. They parted company, Billy to do business and the ladies to buy gowns and take tea, arranging to meet later on Liverpool Street Station. The ladies arrived early and settled themselves in corner seats on the train. Just as the guard was about to blow his whistle, Billy hobbled onto the platform, bare-footed, bowler hat in position, shouting 'Sally m' gel, where are you?' and they had to show themselves, if only to abate the noise.

Sir Edmund Barnard (1856–1930) was another colourful man. He lived on Fair Green, Sawbridgeworth, was a Hertfordshire County Councillor from 1880–1930 and Chairman from 1920–30. He fought various parliamentary by-elections and general elections as a Liberal, in Epping in 1885 and Kidderminster in 1910, defeating Baldwin, the future Prime Minister. Then, defeated as a National Party candidate for East Islington in 1917, he stood for Hertford in the 1918 General Election and lost to Pemberton Billing. An election ditty of that time is still remembered in Bishop's Stortford:

'Vote, vote, vote for Pemberton-Billing
Stick old Barnard in the eye.
Billing's the man, we'll have him if we can.
We won't vote for Barnard any more.'

Ann Fitzgerald, one of 22 children, was born on the Isle of Arran in 1832. Literacy was considered important by islanders so it can be assumed that Ann could read and write. She would have acquired the skills of islanders in weaving and kelp-making, and have endured the hardships and fears of a fishing community where faith and hope were the virtues most in demand. To be banished from such a close-knit people must have been a wrench when Ann married an English soldier and became Mrs White. It is uncertain when she came to Bishop's Stortford, but it is known that she walked on Sunday to Mass at Old Hall Green—a round journey of approximately 16 miles.

50

Whatever she lacked, it was not physical or moral stamina. In 1874, Mass was sometimes available at the home of Dr O'Reilly at 2 Windhill. The Catholic community was then centred in Dunmow.

With the arrival of the Sisters of St Mary of Namur in 1896, baptisms were conferred, first at their house in Grange Road and then at Windhill Lodge where a chaplain was installed, and the Convent became the centre for a small group of Catholics in Bishop's Stortford. Ann White's weekly pilgrimage came to an end. Her daughter, Alice, one of 13 children, married a local man, John Sapsford, in the Convent.

A red-headed boy born in Donegal in 1862 became a tram driver in Glasgow and later a Redemptorist Lay Brother, and as Brother Xavier, first came to Bishop's Stortford in 1900 with Father Vassall-Phillips (1857–1932), to find suitable premises to start a small monastery and church. They settled on No 62 Portland Road, an adequate house with room at the side for a small church, a mobile building, called the 'Tin Tabernacle' by New Towners.

In 1902, in a letter to parishioners, Father Vassall-Phillips reporting on the progress made, referred to the beginning when there were but two faithful families in the parish, an Irish family and a German family. These were Ann White and her family and Mr Fehrenbach and his wife and children, a clock and watchmaker, latterly of Potter Street, Bishop's Stortford, but first established in 1863 in South Street. Ann White died on 30 January 1910 at 23 Bells Hill.

As a young man, Francis Bourne (1861–1935) frequently visited his uncle, Dr Charles Hodson (1885) at The Chantry on his way to St Edmund's College, getting there on horseback. Later he was to become Cardinal Bourne and attended the luncheon for 200 celebrities and parishioners in the Great Hall to celebrate the consecration of the new St Joseph's Church in 1906. The cardinal's hat, that splendid confection of magenta silk, symbol of his authority, was hung as was the custom, over his tomb in St Edmund's College, the tassels much singed by the alter servers' candles.

To the boys of New Town, Brother Xavier was fair game—his ginger hair, the clay pipe, the long black habit, not to mention his rich Donegal accent, all a source of great merriment. 'Pull up Ginger, got a bite?' they would yell when Brother Xavier pulled the Angelus bell. 'Knock down Ginger' took on special significance—knocking at the Monastery door, then running away. Occasionally stones were thrown at the congregation. Brother Xavier hardly took it without protest. However, his robust background in Donegal and Glasgow and native good humour gradually endeared him to Stortfordians.

His first job was to train alter-servers. Young Cecil Ayley was so small, none of the cassocks would fit him. With his usual resourcefulness, Brother Xavier tacked two of his own red handkerchiefs to the bottom of a 'cotta' and Cecil was ready for action. Later, Cecil Ayley was to become a founder member of the local Conservative Club in the Corn Exchange and was well-known locally as 'Doc' Ayley, chemist and dental practitioner in Station Road. In December 1952 when fire broke out at the Monastery there was consternation as Brother Xavier went back into the smouldering hall. 'I've got to save three nuns' he cried, to reappear seconds later with a tin of his favourite tobacco.

While he continued his quiet work as lay brother, many a young priest and raw novice were to benefit from his wise counsel and keen sense of humour. When he was approaching his 98th year, the grand old face crowned with white hair, protruding from under a black skull cap and resting on the collar of his black cape, he looked like a cross between the humourous granny of the Giles cartoons and the kindly old man that he was. If asked, he could probably tell you the latest football results or the score at Lords. Brother Xavier did not achieve his century and was laid to rest in the Monastery garden in 1960.

Sarah or 'Sally' Death (1827–1920), is still rembered as the lady in black with the white stockings. She lived in seclusion in South Lodge, South Road, with blinds drawn so as not to fade the furniture. Tallow candles in silver candelabra were the only light permitted in winter. Rene, one of two daughters of Stephen George Flint, her coachman, groom and gardener, was allowed the freedom of the house under the watchful eye of cook and housemaid. She was to call Miss Death 'Aunt Sarah' when they were alone, otherwise 'Ma'am', a ruse which preserved the social division of the times, a conspiracy that brought them closer together. Rene was instructed in the proper use of cutlery and table manners. The Flints lived in Thorley Lodge, fronting South Road.

Miss Death seldom walked anywhere. She drove in her landau to church in Water Lane and on social occasions, and used a little Victoria on shopping expeditions or to take religious books, once a week, to the old people in the King's Cottages. Her white stockings were well displayed as she descended from her carriages and were a source of local curiosity and comment. Once a year she gave Rene a length of dress material and she was the only child in Hockerill Girls' School to have 'rinking boots', laced half way and studded to the top.

Rene showed musical talent and Sarah Death arranged for her to have piano lessons, first in a large class of 16 in Hugh Villas, and later private tuition; her speech and her manners were

monitored. 'I don't know whose child you are', her mother complained sadly.

In mourning for the death of her uncle, Woodham Death, in 1889, Sarah Death found friendship and comfort in the family of the Congregational Pastor, John Wood (1841–1915). This gentleman of fiery temperament and strong beliefs lived in North Lodge, next to old Northgate School. He was to take over the ministry at a difficult time and was popular for his intellect and organising ability and for his pastoral dedication. The fiery side of his nature was reserved for his liberal politics. He supported Home Rule for Ireland and led the District opposition to the

1902 Education Act and was a passive resister to payment of rates up to 1914. A Hertfordshire County Councillor for six years, he was a member of the Education Committee and he strongly supported the building of the Herts & Essex High School, as well as becoming a governor of Bishop's Stortford College. Conservatives painted his house blue one night, and traces of colour could still be seen under the eaves into the 1930s.

Rev John Wood had two daughters; Kathleen, who boasted that she had a Jesuit cousin and was sent to school in Moravia 'to calm her down', and Norah who later taught piano at Herts & Essex High School.

Rev John Wood was a man of imposing stature. Enveloped in a large black cape, he was invariably accompanied by his dog, a Great Dane, with a lame leg on which it wore a black knitted stocking.

Sarah Death and Kathleen Wood became firm friends. Kathleen often visited South Lodge to view the rare collection of orchids tended by Flint, or to help with the embroidery of beads on cushions of silk and satin and velvet, which were then finished off by the servants and sold for charity.

Miss Death displayed a hidden sense of humour on one memorable visit to Mardon's for stationery. Flint was told to drive the horse round Northgate End out of the sun. Flint went as far as The Grange in Rye Street, but there was no sign of Sarah Death on his return, so he drove round the Corn Exchange, stopping only for the cross passage of carts and tubs. He repeated the performance under the alert eye of Superintendent Foster, who stood at The George corner. 'Why are you driving in circles?' he asked. Flint explained that he was waiting for his mistress. 'A likely story', said the Superintendent, 'Miss Death is sitting up behind you'. She had hopped into the carriage as it waited at the cross-roads and sat there quietly, her hands in her lap, the black skirts draped demurely over the white stockings.

Her nephew, Dr Morris, lived at No 6 Windhill with his sister Hilda, a talented artist who exhibited in the Paris Salon. In 1935, she painted a water colour showing two nuns going up Windhill and Rev William McCarthy coming down, a scene that was little changed from the days when Miss Death visited them in her landau.

At the outbreak of the 1914 War, Rene was left to become a student at Hockerill Training College, but left 'to do her bit' and to help support her parents, as other girls did. She became a Post Office messenger. One snowy winter day found her cycling to Farnham for the Post Office; there were no lights and the snow came up to her knees. She was rescued by cattle drover Tubby Read, who gallantly carried her bicycle above his head all the way back to Bishop's Stortford, while Rene struggled on beside him. As soon as she was old enough she joined Featherby's Works, putting fuses into 20 lb aerial bombs.

Mr Flint became a Special Constable and earned the dislike, even hatred, of the people because of his rigid application of the blackout. Bishop's Stortford lay in the path of the Zeppelin. 'Flint the name, Flint the nature', people said.

Featherby's siren was used as an air raid warning. Once when the Stokes aerial bombs were ready for collection, the Government could not supply the special boxes. Mr Featherby acquired a circular saw and traction engine, bought growing timber, felled it and made his own boxes and delivered the bombs to Woolwich in person.

In 1914-15, the population was increased at one stroke, by 20,000 troops and their horses. All stabling was commandeered and every house had soldiers billeted. The Flints had four and Sarah Death was to accommodate 20 men in her attic, much to her annoyance.

There were several horse stampedes, by King Edward's Horse at Silverleys and the Canadian mules in the Spinney on the Great Hadham Road, as well as by others, doing great damage to property in High Street and Bridge Street. Horses galloped as far as Newport and Epping, carreering into The Chantry at Northgate End and colliding with lamp-posts, severely injuring themselves. What was called 'the great stampede' issued from fields, now the football ground in South Road, where it was said 400 horses belonging to the Royal Staffs Yeomanry were tethered on long ropes. They galloped into the wide ditch which used to divide Stortford from Thorley, near Thorley Lodge, and it was told that 40 horses trampled each other to death. This horrific scene was witnessed by young George Featherby, who lived opposite in No 21 London Road. Conscientious objectors were suspected, but nothing was proven.

It was expected that the town's sewers would fail to support the intake of soldiers, but they survived into our own time. The presence of troops meant morning kit inspection, much to the embarrassment of Miss Parsons of No 52 Portland Road, who had to pick her way through heaps of kit piled on the pavement. Young ladies had to endure the familiar sounds of male approval.

Volunteer Ambulance-man Arthur Muncer was in charge of five ambulances and nursing staff, parked at Wharf House by the old Shades Public House. He drove the wounded men arriving by train, from the station to Egbert Cooper's old house No 2 Half Acres, in use as a temporary hospital. When news of the death in action of Mr Laurie Frere's only son reached Twyford Hamlet, the whole village grieved.

After the war, Rene Flint played the piano at the cinema, accompanying visiting artistes. At Twyford House, the three Misses Frere, Phyllis, Ursula and Beryl, together with their governess, organised country dancing for the young people of Thorley Village and Rene achieved her ambition to play the grand piano. There were swimming lessons in the Stort and the sound of music and laughter once again from the garden of Twyford House.

Rene Flint became Mrs Reed. Now widowed, she lives in Firlands House, still giving pleasure by playing the piano and perpetuating the values she learned from Miss Sally Death at South Lodge.

The Pritchetts were a distinguished family and in their way typical of their times. Mr G.E. Pritchett, architect, had offices in Sawbridgeworth and later in 1874 in North Street, Bishop's Stortford. He found a building site between Green Lane (Cricketfield Lane), Pleasant Road and Chantry Road, bounded by the thornfields to the west. Having acquired it, he had a deep well dug to bring water to the site. It corresponded in importance to the Chantry land on the opposite side of Chantry Road, running north/south from Green Lane to the junction of North Street bounded by Elm Road to the east. To the north were the paddocks and gardens of Whitehall, the home of Tresham Gilbey.

Mr Pritchett had a liking for antiques and the Tudor period in architecture. To achieve the Tudor dimension, he had acquired and accumulated antique fireplaces, timber and other spare parts from period houses, restored or demolished, and used them in the construction of Oak Hall. The original house was completed with a thatched roof. Mr Pritchett was reported to offer to exchange fine new furniture for old, and many a fine old piece changed hands in this manner, destined to adorn the rooms of Oak Hall.

Writing from Oak Hall in 1884 to the *Herts and Essex Observer* Mr Pritchett describes: 'A cottage on the crest of Chantry Road, Bishop's Stortford was upheaved and moved in a most tumultuous manner. The trees around were most perceptively shaken, as were those at Oak Hall. Upon the high ground of Windhill the undulations were strongly felt and the employees in

Messrs Slater's Tayloring Establishment nearby were so alarmed as to find their way downstairs as rapidly as possible'. He was referring to the Great Earthquake of 1884 in Essex.

In the early 1900s, it was disputed whether Mr Pritchett or Mr Harry George Featherby had the first De Dion motor car in Bishop's Stortford. If loud bangs were heard it was presumed to be one of the two gentlemen out for a ride. The De Dion was a noisy single cylinder model which was always breaking down. Mrs Pritchett was confined to an invalid chair drawn by a donkey. It was not unusual to see the De Dion, having spluttered to a halt, being drawn home by the same donkey. Once the two Miss Pritchetts were driving to Stansted and the De Dion would only turn right at Stansted Road. It continued a mad course across Hockerill cross-roads to Hallingbury where it came to a halt and the young ladies had to travel back to Stortford by hay cart.

Mr Pritchett is said to have presented X-ray equipment to Rye Street Hospital. This was kept in a stout chest, in a private ward of the hospital during World War I. Mr Pritchett designed and had the first electric generator installed in the town at Oak Hall. The ruins, fake or real, in the Chantry Garden, now 'Monk's Walk' were attributed to him. Some say they were part of a demolished London Church—Blackfriars perhaps? Others say that they came from old St Michael's, Windhill, at the time of its restoration in the 19th century.

Miss Ursula Pye recalls the beautiful garden of Oak Hall, the tennis court and fine drive to the front door but, best of all, the gardener, Mr Clarke returning from Pritchett's meadow, now Willow Springs, with pails of bubbling warm milk straight from the cows who pastured there.

The Lacy family who lived in Thornfields acquired the deep well and enough land from the Pritchetts for a poultry farm. Mr Pritchett, by then an old, sad and unkempt figure, went into decline and the estate, so proudly begun, started to disintegrate. In 1914, Oak Hall and what remained of the grounds became Army property. Later it was used as a prisoner-of-war camp and prisoners could be seen exercising behind a wired-in compound from the heights of the rhododendron walk to Whitehall. Two prisoners escaped and were recaptured in an open boat off the East Coast.

In 1918, the ex-army/PoW Huts at Oak Hall were in great demand. Mr Duchesne, Bursar at The College, acquired two. Raised on stilts and clad in concrete, they have done duty as houses in Maze Green Road ever since.

Miss Kathleen Hill (1879–1975), known as 'old Kate', washed herself daily in cold water. Latterly she might be seen on Windhill clad in a faded blue pinny polishing the brass knocker on Mr York's door, No 2, or taking a broom sweeping out 'old Granny Hughes'' passage. She belonged to a generation which did good to other people but considered it menial to do their own work. Her beautiful dining table was ever set for four, with

Victorian comport, crystal, silver and napkins, all gathering dust, but ready for the guests who might never come.

Miss Hill was once a debutante who rode to hounds. She also rode on her motorcycle to fires, carrying refreshments with her for the firemen. Once a week she took wine and smoked a clay pipe with Mr Albert Tucker, one-time Captain of the Fire Brigade. She presented the old Fire Brigade with a bell in memory of Fireman James Hart, licensee of The Royal Oak, who was killed falling off the new Leyland Fire Engine on a trial

run in 1935. During the last war she had been a valuable member of the ARP and fire-fighting service.

Miss Hill was keeper of the key to St Michael's Tower, which she would yield only with difficulty and explanation. Neighbouring St Joseph's Church provided spectacle and the Corpus Christi procession was an excuse for a tea party, on a rare occasion when her fine bone china and silver came into use, the lace curtains were drawn back and perhaps a window was opened.

A visit to London would give rise to a discussion as to what to wear: 'Tissiman and his tweeds, Abraham and his seed forever', she would say, donning a well-worn tailored suit. She had been a very smart young lady once and her prayer books were bound in leather to match her tweeds—purple, ivory, crocodile or green. A verger at St Michael's came forward to greet her one Sunday;

'We don't have Vergers for Lent' was an example of her dry wit, disconcerting except to those who knew her.

Her interest in animal welfare was well known. Angry when she met a gipsy whipping his unfortunate horse drawing a heavy load up Windhill, she snatched the whip, released the horse, tethered him to a tree outside the Monastery and told the protesting, bewildered man to get into harness and she would drive him and the load to its destination. 'Isaac and his seven sons' were evacuee cats abandoned in Vyse Court. They developed cat 'flu, but cradled in shoe boxes, they were nursed back to health by Miss Hill. She walked about the town, a cat napping on her shoulders, and in her pantry window hung several cat tails, whether as a deterrent to mice or men, we shall never know.

Callers were invited into morning room or drawing room, and visitors were kept firmly apart. When she died, many bequests of silver and ornaments to friends were never realised—burglars took care of that. St Michael's Church received two chairs, originally ecclesiastical furniture. At the end, her proud head was bowed when she had to submit to being fed by a neighbour. 'I think the time has come to call me Kathleen' she said.

There was no holding back the passage of time or its social customs for the Blake family who were caught on the changing tide. John Blake married Hilda Jean from Aberdeen in 1928. They were then housekeeper and butler to a member of the Lyle family on the Hogsback, Guildford, and came in the same capacity to the Langham family of Hadham Place, where there were already five maids in the household. The family were dairy wholesalers and although the young couple could have had as much skimmed milk as they wanted for their baby, they preferred to walk into Bishop's Stortford to buy a branded baby food prescribed by their doctor. The walk proved too much for them as there were no 'buses in 1928. (As late as 1932, the Bishop's Stortford UDC spent a whole year debating whether to change over from horse-drawn Council transport to motorised vehicles.) The Blakes accepted the chance of transferring to Church Manor, as housekeeper and butler to Mr Rose, one-time American Ambassador to China. They had hardly settled into a comfortable routine when the gold crash ruined Mr Rose and he had to return home.

Homeless and unemployed, they were fortunate to find a house on Thorley Hill at 25 shillings per week rent. Mrs Blake took in lodgers, young draughtsmen at Millar's Works, and made one penny buns and sixpenny currant cakes, which John Blake trundled round the houses on a home-made barrow. One night there was a fearful storm which swelled an underground spring over which the house was built and the whole corner fell away, leaving young John precariously perched in his cot in the gaping dark, his parents frightened but otherwise safe.

They removed to a house in Grange Road with eight rooms, six with bell-pulls and working bells in the kitchen, a back staircase 'for the servants' but no bathroom, at a rent of 28

shillings per week. John Blake started work at once offering 'Blakies Cakies'. When the bright young lodgers arrived, it was made quite plain by a neighbour that they were 'letting down the neighbourhood', and when three young men hammered on her door after a night out, singing 'Show me the way to go home', it was the last straw. However, upon learning about the Blakes' dwindling savings and their trials, she proved most understanding and tolerant.

Glasscocks the bakers then developed confectionery and that was the end of the 'cakies' except at the young men's 'Welcome Club' over Sullivan's Antique Shop in South Street, where John Blake was sure of a sell out.

The changing social and economic scene suggested a new need for part-time domestic service for home entertaining. The Blakes were once more active as a team, possibly the first 'flying cook and butler'. For ten shillings an evening, they would lay the table, cook and wash up and serve, regardless of the number of guests involved.

John Blake secured a permanent part-time job as valet and butler to Mr Laurie Frere at Twyford House for nine years. By then an invalid, Mr Frere rarely dressed beyond changing pyjamas and dressing gown. With John Blake to help him, he led a tolerably independent life. In summer he enjoyed the encroaching wilderness of the garden, painting water-colours. He had unsuccessfully submitted work to the Royal Academy for 34 years. Mr Frere added a new dimension to the beneficence of his family to the town by encouraging John Blake to sketch the decaying beauty of the past, those hidden corners of Bishop's Stortford, many now crumbled away.

When Mr Frere died in 1939, he left John Blake £1 per year of service, according to the custom. Thus ended, upon the division of the estate, the occupation of Twyford House by two related families after a tenure of 250 years. During World War II, it became a Maternity Home and 693 babies were born there. Now after a period of decrepitude and vandalism, it is due for rehabilitation.

Miss Dick's civic menu card.

ABOVE: The Congregational Church, Water Lane in a print of 20 September 1860 and BELOW: Hockerill and the railway from The Mound (Castle Field), in a print dated 14 February 1861.

ABOVE: Good Friday fish displayed at Powell's by Billy Peck. INSET: Brother Xavier. BELOW: St Joseph's, Portland Road 'Tin Tabernacle', 1900.

Il Padre P. R. Philipps Vassall implora per sè e per i fedeli della sua Parrocchia Bishops Stortford l'Apostolica Benedizione.

*His Holiness the Pope receives Father Vassall-Phillips' petition
for the Apostolic Blessing on priest and parish.*

*LEFT: Algernon Talmadge assists Harry Sparrow in W.
Playle's 19th century moving study and RIGHT: Miss Sally
Death sits for a formal portrait, while BELOW: she relaxes
in the garden at South Lodge, attended by coachman G. Flint.*

Rev W. McCarthy approaches as two nuns move away, in this
study of High Street and Windhill by Hilda Morris in 1935.

ABOVE: Twyford House by Buckler. CENTRE: Rev John Wood's British School, (Northgate Activities Centre). BELOW: Mr Pritchett's Oak Hall.

*ABOVE: The Cemetery Lodge designed by G. E. Pritchett,
now the Local History Museum. BELOW: The Procession
passes Miss Hill's house.*

ABOVE: Men of the Royal Scots billeted on the Bakers of Water Lane in 1915. (Reg Baker in the sailor-boy outfit).
BELOW: H. Sparrow Ltd, North Street, puts out the flags for Peace celebrations in 1919.

MADE BY HAND

The last century brought a remarkable upsurge in church congregations. With the exception of St Michael's, much renovated in the nineteenth century, nearly all Bishop's Stortford's churches were built or commenced before the turn of the century.

Mr G. E. Pritchett, architect and son of the Rector of Great Hallingbury, was commissioned to draw up the plans for old All Saints' Church, Hockerill, in Gothic style. All Saints was commenced in 1851, to be gutted by a terrible fire in 1935. Another building designed by Mr Pritchett was the Cemetery Lodge.

The erection of the Corn Exchange was commenced 1828 after a design by Vulliamy; it dwarfed the older but smaller buildings in the Market Square.

Public sculpture in Bishop's Stortford is almost entirely confined to churches and memorials and a stone statue on St Joseph's School wall. Yet a fine example of cut stone is apparent over the chemist's shop on the east side of North Street, formerly known as Speechly and Milbank. The stone carvings represent the herbs used in pharmacy. The stone was hand-cut on the pavement and then placed in position.

The 19th century saw the beginning of a building boom that was to continue for over half a century. Local artisans and craftsmen enjoyed regular employment and the chance to acquire new skills and knowledge. Small wonder that Puper Lilley, a bricklayer from New Town, contrived to walk his dog on Windhill in 1906 as the congregation was coming out of St Joseph's or the 'Italian Mission' as it was called. He raised his hand dramatically and called out 'I helped to build this Church, I helped to build this Church'. When the final slate was hung on the Convent roof, a man thrust himself down the tall chimney and waved his legs in the air.

The famous graffiti-ists of 1820 left the mark of their discontent at the meanness of the church wardens for not allowing them a ration of beer on St Michael's Church Tower. This legend on the west face is discernible from the attic windows of the Monastery.

James Amos Ashwell, of Stortford Park Farm, Bishop's Stortford signed an Indenture made in August 1868 between his son, Arthur Ashwell and Francis Richard Crick, clock and watchmaker of North Street. Francis R. Crick was to be paid £50 in two instalments and to instruct the apprentice over a period of $4\frac{1}{2}$ years. Further, Arthur Ashwell was to learn all practices conducive to running a good business and was to have the same food and eat at the same table as the Crick family.

Arthur Ashwell did well. He took over the business when F. Crick emigrated to Canada, and removed to No 22 North Street, the deeds of which premises go back to 1697. Arthur Ashwell conserved the carved doors and fine banisters of the old building, erecting a new brick facade.

The family were to assume the care of St Michael's clock over three generations. The clock bears the legend 'John Bryant fecit 1820'. J. Bryant was a bell caster of Hertford noted for his skill as a clockmaker. The clock is described by F. Ashwell as being of the 'Birdcage' type, the works contained in a framework of iron stays and struts. It is believed to have the longest pendulum and largest weight for miles; the leaden weight weighs a quarter of a ton with an 80 feet drop. It used to be wound up by the Ashwells twice weekly. The north and south dials were added in 1846 by James Yardley of Bishop's Stortford. There is evidence of an older church clock going back to 1431, and later mention of a campanelium. By 1607 the hours were struck on the tenor bell and chimes were fitted. Other old clocks to survive in the town are those of Benskins, Church Manor and the Bargee's clock now facing Dane Street on the wall of 2, Hockerill Street.

A clock bearing the name of Francis Crick still ticks away on the mantlepiece of a house on Windhill; another was fixed to an inside wall of the Westminster Bank until post-war renovations.

Some builders specialised in the erection of public buildings; others have served the need for housing. One such firm was F. Cannon & Sons in New Town over 100 years ago. When Mrs Arthur Church of Bishop's Stortford first glimpsed the ancient sea port of Boulogne with its houses rising to the ramparts around the splendid domed Cathedral, she was heard to say 'It needs Cannon's men on it'. This sums up the regard in which local people held this family firm of builders, which has been active in Bishop's Stortford for almost 150 years. Before that the Cannon family were engaged in carpentry, as recorded since 1800. Indeed the skill of Stortford carpenters was well known to the Bishop of London even in 1396, when he sent to Bishop's Stortford for skilled men to advise him on the reconstruction of Crachehegh Mill in Hackney; they were to extract old timber and prepare the great beam.

On 24 May 1897, the *Herts & Essex Observer* printed a notice by Eliza Cannon thanking customers for their continued support over the previous 25 years and assuring them that she would continue in the building business with her son, Frederick, as Manager. Women have had a place in the administration ever since.

Susan Cannon, born 1965, assumed the role of family historian; she wrote a detailed account of family and business activities for a school project. 'Patriarch' Frederick insisted that his property should be rented by railway men; as they were regularly employed, that ensured prompt payment of rent. So it was believed that New Town was built solely for railway workmen. Cannon houses were built to last. Money raised from the building and sale of Highland House, Dunmow Road financed the building of Sidney Terrace, so called after the first baby to be born there, the son of a railway man, Mr Challis. Only hand-made bricks were used in Cannon houses up to 1933, latterly from Bedlars Green Brickfield which was formerly part of the Houblin Estate. After 1933, they were machine-made at the Start Hill Brickworks.

In the new Cemetery stands an old pump operated by a tap; the long pumping handle has gone and watering cans have replaced the horse trough which once stood underneath; birds hatch their young in the hole left by the pump handle. Once it stood in North Street and offered a cool drink, fed from a well under the road which was inspected via a chamber with access from the cellar of No 11 North Street. According to Mr J. Cooper who lived there, it was an evil-smelling passage and he kept out of it. From 1839-1914, 11 North Street had been a chemist's shop. Three of the owners, Morse, Hardy and Ecclestone had issued their own 'pots' with lids decorated by Pratt. These are much in demand by collectors.

Memories of South Street in the 1920s recall the tall stooping figure of grey haired, bearded Grandfather Herbert Bacon, an unusual but commanding figure dressed in tweed knickerbockers, Norfolk jacket and small brimmed cap. His policeman father served in Norfolk, Newport and Stansted, where he apprenticed Herbert to Daniel Robinson in the plumbing and building trade. After the first world war, father and son formed a building partnership, first in New Town Road and then in the stables where Sir Walter Gilbey formerly kept his polo ponies on the railway paddocks, Station Road, Bishop's Stortford.

It was often necessary to ensure a water supply outside the system so the Bacons called in a water diviner, until Herbert decided to become a dowser. He was thrilled to discover that it took all his strength to control the hazel fork. He predicted correctly that the South Street sewer was laid in running sand and would disintegrate, and he traced the source of Bishop's Stortford's water supply, concluding that the town had an underground lake. He could calculate the depth of water and its course. While instruments achieve an accurate result today, the general knowledge and natural skills of water diviners were important then.

Herbert Bacon won a national competition for water divining and made the columns of the national press—he was invited to find buried treasure on a London estate, but declined. This dignified man was nicknamed 'Porky Bacon' or 'Ham Rinds'; perhaps the names were a device by which New Towners in those days came to terms with Herbert's unusual talent. He has been described as an able and accurate architect and draughtsman by Mr 'Jock' Elliott, who as a young man worked with Mr Bacon and appreciated his thoroughness. Jock Elliott was later to found the local building firm of J. A. Elliott Ltd.

Herbert Bacon was particularly susceptible to thundery weather and reacted in such a manner that he had to be secured when working on scaffolding. Local artist John Blake tells how his small son, aged 3 years, saw the bearded Mr Bacon coming up Thorley Hill and called out that 'Jesus Christ was coming up the hill on a bicycle'. Certainly one might have been excused for mistaking him for Moses with the tablets, as he worked on a coping stone to the rumble of thunder.

Joseph Dorrington Day of South Street, builder and stone mason, made an important discovery when preparing a site for a house in Maple Avenue; he found the bones of a large animal said to be an Iron Age horse. On the advice of Dr Irving, naturalist and Vicar of all Saints', Hockerill, a large covered area, part of a carpenter's shop, was made available to them by

Mr Harry George Featherby at his works on London Road (now Millar's Works). The bones, carefully collected, preserved and reassembled there, then went on display in the Natural History Museum for a number of years.

Joseph Day's daughter, Daisy Day, became a household name, noted for her photographic child studies in the '20s and '30s. Her father had agreed to her having a profession of her own, and attracted to the photography course at the London Polytechnic, and inspired by the success of Miss Eva Barrett, who was making an international name for herself, she persuaded a reluctant Joseph Day to set up a studio for her and he became her patient and tolerant model. One of her most beautiful pictures is a study of him playing chess with his friend Mr Carver.

Other important craftsmen of the time were the 'Snobs', who made footwear and harnesses.

In the '30s, on a small elevated area of land between the Half Moon's stables and Dodd's, the dentists, stood three cottages and a workshop. The area is now a flower bed backed by a hoarding. Yet, from 1830, the single storey workshop was a hive of industry. Lit by an oil lamp and heated by coal, it was a cosy place where the smell of warm pliant leather pervaded and three generations of the Mills family plied their trade.

Mr George Mills (1870-1957) is remembered as much for his human kindness as for his skill with the heel ball and sole ball irons, heated by candle flame and applied to make the edges of shoes and boots smooth and shiny. He lived at Hatfield Heath; dressed in black bowler and pin-stripe trousers, he used to walk there and back, an hour either way, until he married a maid at The Chantry and moved into the cottage beside his workshop.

The boots and shoes were made by hand. A Frenchman, a cripple, needed specially light shoes. Mr Mills used wooden pegs no thicker than a match stick to achieve the result. Eventually, the machine-made articles made hand shoe-making uneconomic. A one-time neighbour, now past her half century, recalls with what fascination she watched Mr Mills put on his leather apron and transfer his skills into working footwear and delicate shoes. As she watched the waxing of the threads, it was not only the material warmth of the place she experienced, but Mr Mills' great kindness of heart. With a family to support and money scarce, he knew when a shovelful of coal might come in handy to cook a neighbour's Sunday dinner, or half-a-crown would stave off hunger for a family until pay day.

Carvings created for Speechley and Milbank, chemists.

LEFT: Alice Crick in her wedding hat and RIGHT: clockmaker Francis Crick of North Street. BELOW: Paris 'bus bought by J. A. Elliott Ltd for town twinning events, here in a special Giles cartoon. (Reproduced by permission of J. A. Elliott Ltd).

Pot lids by Pratt for three Stortford chemists.

ABOVE: Daisy Day's study of Mr Carver and her father Dorrington Day. BELOW: 1 October 1851 engraving of the old Hockerill Church – All Saints'.

LEFT: Child Study *by Daisy Day. RIGHT: Gateway to the Chantry. BELOW: Hadham Road with the Chantry on the left, Amos Pryer's premises ahead and Mr Mills' workshop just out of sight behind the roses on the right.*

SONS OF THE SOIL

Gerald Scott, born in 1888 in the last house in Apton Road, went to live with the Gillett family in Little Hadham, attending the village school, to which he took a short cut through the osier beds, regarded by him as his secret world where he knew every bird and every tree. One day, young Fred Ashwell, then about 17 years old, and his cousin Percy were inspecting the wood as a possible camp site for Fred's Scouting Troop. They asked Gerald why he was trespassing on Ashwell land. It seemed the osier beds were not his domain after all.

The Scouts departed; then in the early 1900s, Gerald found that he was the youngest gamekeeper, at least in those parts, thanks to old Dr Morris, old Alfred Nockolds, (1847-1928), 'Goldie' Hall and Tom Cornwell—four sporting gentlemen from Bishop's Stortford. They hired the shooting rights in the osier beds from the Ashwells and Gerald was paid three shillings for a whole Saturday's work and given four bottles of ginger beer. He was also given corn to entice pheasants into the woods. Gerald laid a corn trail onto land owned by the Duke of Wellington and soon the osier beds were well stocked with pheasant. Hampers of fine food were left at the Gillett's for the weekly shoot and Gerald dined well on the leftover delicacies.

Mr Jackson, coach proprietor, who operated a cab service from his stables on the Rye Street/Barrells Down Road corner to the Station, drove the four gentlemen and their gardeners to and from Little Hadham.

Gerald Scott was one day to rear pedigree hens. The poultry was exported to 50 countries and Mr Scott supplied 11 governments.

In the 1920s, Mr Brace from Cox's farm, Great Havers was a cheery, familiar figure in his gleaming milk float, as rotund himself as the churns beside him. His whistling could be heard above the trotting hooves of his horse and the clang of his shining pint and half-pint measure pots brought his customers to the door with their milk jugs and an occasional cup of tea for the milkman.

The Firmin girls, each carrying a churn on the front of a bicycle, would be on their round in South Road and South Mill, setting out from their home near The Jolly Brewers.

It was the heyday of the private milkman. The Thickings family had kept cows in New Town in 1874. George Thickings and his brother grazed cows in the Meads, in Hockerill Fields (now King's Court) and in meadows east and west of Parsonage Lane. Up to the last war, the cattle were driven home through the town to Castle Street, where they were milked and bedded during the winter. In summer they were driven to and fro twice a day. The lowing of cows was as familiar around Trinity Street as the sound of cart wheels and the cock's crow. Milking at Plaw Hatch under the trees may seem idyllic, but occasional bird droppings or the odd fly found their way into the milk. In Portland Road, the Thickings Brothers were likely to encounter young Archie Parsons from No 52, a clerk with Alliance Insurance in the City. Always late, rushing to catch his train, 'What time is it?', he would call out. 'Keep on running and I will tell you, Sir,' would be the answer. Milk then was rich in cream.

During the war years the 'Jubber' Thickings were a welcome sight in Parsonage Lane, jogging along to Plaw Hatch, with the churns up behind. One got the impression that whatever stopped, the Jubbers would go on forever, caps well down on their ears, wing-collared 'dickies' in place over their flannel shirts, clay pipes gripped between their teeth and the pony's head down, drawing the little cart, its human load bobbing up and down in rhythm with the wheels. It was a way of life, hard-working and independent. Its constancy was reassuring when the peace of Parsonage Lane, then fronted by a few houses, was broken by the thunder of tanks and armoured divisions on endless missions to preserve that same independence.

The Jubbers made one concession to winter—a slit sack over their heads, covering their backs. As a white film of frost enveloped the hairy covering, the vision suggested some strange winter ghosts from the hoary depths of Birchanger Woods. One day there were three 'pixie' hoods of sacking; the Jubber Thickings had acquired an evacuee. She was to stay with them for the 'duration' and to visit them for many years afterwards

The children of Parsonage Lane had a skipping rhyme that went like this: 'Do you like foxes, Do you like chickens, Do you like kissing old Jubber Thickings?'

82

During the depression in the 1920s many an arable farmer turned to dairy farming from economic necessity.

Mr Toby Harvey, who followed his father at Exnalls Farm, Much Hadham, recalls how his father Jack Harvey delivered his milk daily to London during the general strike in 1926, taking with him an ash stick for self defence, if necessary; this was hollowed out and weighted with lead.

The Harvey family had been farmers since the early part of 1700. Toby Harvey's grandfather farmed Stortford Park, and his father used to ride into Stortford to school at The College, stabling his pony at The Bricklayer's Arms.

The pasteurisation of milk started before the 1939 war in a small way, helped along by the demand of the American Forces for treated milk, aptly called by local farmers 'Paralysed Milk'. Before the development of TT herds and markets, Drs Gammie and Sharpe held weekly surgeries in Bishop's Stortford for bovine tuberculosis in children, now a scourge of the past.

In the inter-war years, adults with tuberculosis often lived in open voluntary isolation. One such was Mr Hales of South Road in the late 1920s, who lived in a greenhouse at the top of his garden near the path which ran from South Road to Thorley Hill, commonly called Sally Death's Passage. In 1933 Father Riley lived in a hut in the Monastery garden, going indoors during the worst winter weather. In the 1940s a young gipsy girl slept out in the open on an iron bedstead in Willett's Field, situated between Heath Row and Parsonage Lane. One sad evening a group of gipsies escorted the young girl to the old Waggon and Horses which stood in a garden opposite Parsonage Lane. It was a heart-chilling thought that she was not just having a last birthday drink, but carrying TB in its final throes into a public drinking place. When she died, her bedding and all personal effects were committed to a huge bonfire. Over forty cars and trucks converged on Parsonage Lane to mourn her. By the light of the bonfire, in the words of a neighbour with a full view of the scene 'Her grandmother took her from her coffin and nursed her, rocking to and fro' "acombing of her hair".'

There were two isolation hospitals for the treatment of small-pox and serious fevers: one on the Great Hadham Road in a field belonging to Castle Farm, and the other in Haymeads Lane. Both have long since disappeared. Visitors rang a bell and were allowed to hand over gifts for the patients to the gatekeeper.

The surrounding countryside was once an important growing area for trifolium and white and red clover. The need for hay finished with the passing of the working farm horse and horse-drawn transport.

Pope and Chapman were seed and cleaning merchants and millers of trifolium, first at Hockerill Street in old Maltings, (severed by the coming of the railway in 1842), later in South Street. George Frederick Chapman (1869-1968), a Cornishman, joined Mr Pope in Mark Lane, London. Of farming stock, he moved back into the country in 1914 as a seed merchant in Bishop's Stortford. Much business was done at the Corn Exchanges in Kings Lynn, Boston and Norwich. A two-way market developed with the Continent. Between two disastrous fires, the South Street premises were used solely for the production of trefoil seed, most of which went to Holland to sow land which had been flooded by the Dutch against German occupation, and later the Polders land reclaimed by the Dutch from the sea. After the second fire, the firm changed over to the mixing and dispatching of grass seed. The fields which once cropped trifolium are now a blinding stretch of yellow rape seed to satisfy our growing consumption of margarine and certain processes in the steel industry.

At 19 Hockerill Street, Frank Chapman has successfully adapted to present day needs. Semi-retired in Furneux Pelham he came to even closer terms with nature by falling into a disused cesspit. Happily he survived the immersion and can truly be called 'a son of the soil'.

Frank Chapman rated Henry Percival Morley the most interesting man he knew. An allround sportsman, Henry was to make an impact on amateur dramatics and operatics in the town (1928-1947) and a name in athletics. He refereed the final England v Rest (Amateurs) in 1926. This was all the more remarkable as he was strictly brought up by Plymouth Brethren parents who discouraged all sport. As a boy he was known to have cut down a pair of trousers for football shorts. His great achievement was the perfecting and patenting of 'the Morley

Process' marketed as 'The London Hospital Surgical Catgut'.

First a chemist's assistant, then a branch manager, in 1911, Henry, at a salary of £100 per annum, was appointed theatre assistant at the London Hospital. He was twice refused Army service in 1914/15. Heavy casualties from the front meant long hours of work in the theatres and 'living in' most weekends to deal with casualty trains. His life is a story of hard grind and sure progress. Success came when as the result of careful observation that successful operations sometimes went wrong, he developed his own formulae for a safe suture. Other hospitals were soon asking for catgut by the 'Morley Process'. Married with a family, he had no money to finance laboratories, so he gave his process to the governors of the London Hospital, who started the project off with 20 staff in 1919.

As the Second World War loomed, there was enormous demand for the product from the Crown Colonies, Dominions and Egypt. In 1940 during the Blitz, the costly equipment used for the final processing was moved from the East End, together with staff, to the Golf Club, Stortford at 48 hours' notice.

ABOVE: Entrance to the Meads. BELOW: Mr Scraggs
and Mr Cutmore on their milk round.

*LEFT: Thorley Fields in 1933, and RIGHT: Father Riley's
hut that same year. CENTRE: H. P. Morley. BELOW:
East view of the fountain, Hockerill, c1905.*

ABOVE: Ironmonger Sworder's staff, late 1890s and
BELOW: Boardman's Victorian facade.

Lot 20.

CONSISTS OF A COMPACT AND TRULY DESIRABLE FARM,

CALLED OR KNOWN AS

Upwicke Farm,

In the Parish of ALBURY, near to BISHOP STORTFORD, HERTS.

Comprising

A good Farm-House, with excellent Barns, Stable, Cow-House, and other requisite Out-Buildings

TOGETHER WITH

FIFTY-TWO ACRES

Of Rich Inclosed, Freehold, Pasture and Arable

LAND;

And TWENTY-FIVE ACRES, 3 ROODS, of Productive Open Field Ditto,

(A small Part of which is Copyhold,)

IN THE FOLLOWING PIECES OR PARCELS:

	ARABLE.			PASTURE.			Total Contents (more or less.)		
	A.	R.	P.	A.	R.	P.	A.	R.	P.
Farm-House, Homestall, Yard, and Pightle......				1	1	3			
The Home Field	15	2	0						
The Grove				1	0	22			
The Nine-Acres	9	2	24						
Long Meadow				4	0	16			
Moors' Meadow.............................				4	1	21			
The Five-Acres	5	1	9						
The Three-Acres	3	1	33						
Hobbs' Hole and the Water-Pightle				1	2	2			
The Home Close and Sable Croft Mead				4	1	22			
	36	3	26	16	3	6	53	2	32
Dispersed in the Open Fields.									
In Mill Field, lying in Six Pieces	18	2	15						
In Great Moor Field, a fine Piece or Parcel of Land	2	3	24						
In Little Moor Field, One other Piece of ditto	1	1	16						
In Patmore Field, Two Pieces of ditto	2	3	7						
	25	2	22				25	2	22
Total Quantity							79	1	14

Land-Tax....	£.8 8 0
Quit-Rent......	0 2 0
	£.8 10 0

The Buildings, Gates, and Fences have lately, at a great Expence, been put in perfect Order, and the Land is in a high State of Cultivation; in the Occupation of Mr. JOHN HOY, at the very low and improvable Rent of £64. per Annum; forming a desirable Opportunity for Investment.

Mr. HOY, the Tenant, will show the Premises.

Details of an 1827 land auction: lot 20, Upwicke Farm.

This is the last Will and Testament of me William Clark of Bishop Stortford in the County of Hertford Ostler. I Give and Devise All my Messuages Lands Tenements Malting Office hereditaments and premises and shares in Messuages Lands Tenements Malting Office hereditaments and premises and all other my real Estate whatsoever and wheresoever unto my Sisters Mary Read and Ruth Collinson their heirs and assigns as Tenants in common and not as joint Tenants. I Give unto my said Sisters all my personal Estate and I appoint them Executrixes of this my Will In witness whereof I the said William Clark have hereunto set my hand this fifteenth day of April one thousand eight hundred and forty eight.

Signed by the said William Clark as and for his last Will and Testament in the presence of us being present and attesting such Signature at the same time who in his presence at his request and in the presence of each other have hereunto set our names as witnesses

Henry Cribb
Surgeon
Bishops Stortford

William Fe

The Mark of

X

William Clark

William Clark's last will and testament, 1848.

QUEEN'S WEATHER

In 1896 Queen Victoria's Diamond Jubilee was celebrated in great style. At 6 am, students in Hockerill Training College were awakened by a sound they thought was gunfire. It was the boom of maroons set off by Mr A.S. Barrett in the town meads, at intervals until 8 am; then came a merry peal of bells from St Michael's.

The singing of the National Anthem and Bishop Wakefield's Hymn at 9 am preceded the planting of a Jubilee oak tree. The students then watched 'a goodly procession of decorated bicycles and carts for prizes' in the town. The afternoon was spent in the leafy backwater of Twyford House, at Mr Laurie Frere's invitation, where there were croquet and tennis and boating on the river. Tea was served in the scented garden, followed by bicycle races on the college machines, which had been brought over by cart. It was a hot summer afternoon—'Queen's weather', they said. Then with bonnets and long summer dresses patted and smoothed to uniform requirements, it was time to go home.

The *College Magazine* describes the tastefully decorated town, the fairy lights, chinese lanterns, the new electric light and the illuminated bicycle procession described as 'weird but strangely attractive'. The day ended with a final rendering of God Save the Queen on the College lawn at 10.30pm.

Bishop's Stortford was evidently the hub of the countryside, with Colonel Houblin of Hallingbury Place, Herbert Sworder, John Barker of Barkers of Kensington, and J.L. Glasscock, the town historian, as the main organising committee.

Gifts and vouchers for the poor were nicely graded: all married couples over 60 years received five shillings; a similar amount went to those on parish relief and to the sick or the very poor. A grocery voucher was given to each widow or widower, spinster or bachelor over 60 years—it came to a total of £70 between 370 people.

Celebrations lasted from 6 am to midnight. Bandsman Pepper took the solo in North Street, and the Band then marched to the meads where a 'Feu de Joie' was fired, followed by cheers for Her Majesty led by Major Williams. Mrs Marshall-Taylor, wife of the Chairman of the UDC, planted a Cedrus Atlantica on the top of Windhill. A strong smell of gas came from the hole, yet it survived.

At 2 pm a huge procession moved towards Silverleys, lent for the occasion by Sir Walter Gilbey for sporting activities. Tea was provided for 1,600 children. By 9 o'clock, North Street and Market Square were well illuminated. In South Street, Joseph Dorrington Day erected a miniature castle on a pretty rockery with a quotation from Tennison: 'She wrought her people lasting good'. The Jubilee bonfire was on a field on the Great Hadham Road by Claypits Farm, presently St Joseph's School site, where 400 faggotts, loads of wood, a barrel of paraffin and a barrel of tar made an awesome blaze at 10 pm. Midnight brought an end to a memorable day for the town.

Bishop's Stortford greeted the Coronation of Edward VII with a blaze of colour. Patriotism and moral scruples were not unmixed on this occasion. 'Righteousness exalteth a Nation, but sin is an offence to any man' was the message combined with 'Good wishes for the Flower Show' and suitable emblems of loyalty to the Crown, which adorned the large front of Barrett's shop in North Street. Joscelyne's had an impressive show of 2,000 paper roses made by the staff, depicting the names of Edward and Alexandra in colourful sequence. The streets converging on North Street were a rainbow of bunting and congratulations.

F. Cannon & Sons, Hockerill Street, erected an archway across the road, festooned with greenery, flowers and Royal tokens. The male staff was photographed with the Cannon family, 'Bill', the youngest, clad in knee length knickerbockers and hard, high collar and small cap. They too stretched across the road. The picture conjures up the peace and relative quiet of such an important road in those days. Today, cars would have tailed back to the crossroads in either direction.

Through the festive arch could be seen The Black Bull public house, and beyond, a narrow neck of lane bounded by maltings to the west. This was then Dane Street. The maltings were pulled down in the '20s to make this into a thoroughfare and the main road to the railway station, joining up with the station bridge which was built by subscription in 1864. Before that, crossing the river had been by ferry.

Edward VII was a frequent passerby on his way to Easton Lodge to relax in the company of his friend, the Countess of Warwick, who was famous for her outspoken Socialism. He was driven by Charles Clarke, coachman from The Chequers. He often drove through to the Newmarket Races, or when visiting his friend, Sir Walter Gilbey, who lived at Elsenham Hall.

Accounts of one noteworthy visit to the town centre vary. Edward VII was expected by the Town Council to pass through North Street. A suitably decorated platform was erected over the

pavement outside the Council Office, that part of the Westminster Bank next to The George Stables, now a dress shop. It was not unusual to see a horse's head sticking out of the upper window in the stable loft. In the 1930s, *The Daily Telegraph* printed a picture of Captain Palmer's Hunter, 'Artful Joe', looking out with almost a smile on his face. On the Royal occasion, local notabilities were given pride of place with the Council to greet the Royal passage through the town. Edward VII was an hour late. The story is really about a Council, which thought it had time for some bracing refreshment and retreated, either into the Council Office, or The George. One story tells how the King arrived and, noticing the empty platform, ordered the Royal coachman to drive on quickly. The other version suggests that Edward VII, already an hour late, would have missed the first race at Newmarket had he taken the town route, so he ordered the Royal coachman to take the A11, thus by-passing the town.

In South Street and South Road, almshouses dedicated during two reigns, the King's Cottages were made available to the elderly poor born in Bishop's Stortford by the generosity of the Gilbey and Vander-Meulen families and by Georgina Menet. When the King's Head medallion was unveiled in 1907, it was found to be facing the wrong way. What must have been a considerable embarrassment to Admiral Vander-Meulen has become a local curiosity.

In 1915, His Majesty King George V reviewed the 2/24th London Regiment at Hallingbury Place, attended by the Principal, staff and students of Hockerill Training College, who had entertained and billeted the troops.

The Queen Mother, as Duchess of York, opened the new Wing of Rye Street Hospital in the '20s. Presented with a bouquet, she had nowhere to put it, so Joe Brazier stepped forward and 'I'll take it Miss' he said gallantly. 'That is very kind of you Mr Brazier', the smiling Duchess replied. As Queen Mother she descended by helicopter on the Bishop's Stortford College Field for the Centenary celebrations in 1968. The helicopter circled so that she could wave to St Joseph's Primary School children on the hill. Princess Margaret visited Hockerill Training College for its centenary.

Twyford House in 1930.

94

ABOVE: *Hockerill Training College, in a print dated 14 February 1861.* CENTRE: *Windhill with the* Cedrus Atlantica *flourishing within its enclosure in 1906.* BELOW: *Procession for Edward VII's Coronation passing the Plume of Feathers, now Joscelyne's.*

ABOVE: *The procession in South Street and* BELOW: *the crowd awaits the spectacle outside Alfred Slaps Barrett's emporium.*

ABOVE: Mr Cutmore, with an effigy of Kaiser Bill in the
1919 Peace celebrations. BELOW: Waiting for Edward
VII's visit to the town.

ABOVE: *The King drives through Market Street towards North Street and BELOW: the archway of firemen's ladders in North Street.*

ABOVE: The George V Coronation Committee, 22 June 1911, CENTRE: their Pageant that day and BELOW: the Parade.

ABOVE: Joe Brazier and dog (right) attend the Royal Proclamation of George V's death. Also pictured: E. G. Cooper, Mr and Mrs T. Gilbey, Mr Tee and N. Drinkwater, Clerk to the UDC. BELOW: The Duchess of York (HM the Queen Mother) arrives to open a new wing of the Rye Street Hospital.

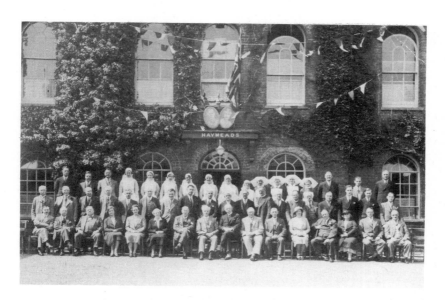

ABOVE: Haymeads staff assemble for the Coronation of George VI. BELOW: HRH Princess Margaret attends the Centenary of Hockerill Training College.

A 'right royal' occasion for Stortford: town twinning with Friedberg-Hessen and Villirs-sur-Marne in 1971. ABOVE: UDC Chairman Cllr Mrs Gee Mason clasps hands with Burgermeister Raute and M. le Maire Roue and BELOW: a tripartite civic ballgame.

MARKET DAYS

Market day in North Street was an exciting affair. Many of the stallholders were local men. The progress of cattle and sheep to Sworder's Market added sound to scent, and excitement to the occasion. The 'bull in the china shop' was all too probable a hazard.

Cattle drovers were men apart. Armed with a long stick they could be relied upon to drive animals to market without injury to property or bystanders or hurt to themselves or to the cattle, through a town crowded with stalls and people. The noise made by seemingly crazed creatures, coupled with the cries of drovers was a fearsome duet, which at once excited and repelled. After the sale, cattle often bolted home again. A beast was not easy to identify once mixed with the herd, thus creating angry argument and confusion once the sale was completed. A drover had to keep a sharp eye on his cattle between weighing machine and market gate. Drover Jack Whiffen was gored more than once. Bullocks driven down South Street by Drover Batsy Thurgood turned tail and made for the stationery shop opposite Apton Road, causing indescribable mess and panic. There were stick fights between drovers, usually fought over disputed territory. Up to the early '20s, Dane Street saw many a stick fight along its sloping, slippery, cobbled way. It was so narrow that a hay cart passing through left straw in the gutters. Windows were continually broken by sparring drovers.

The story goes that when Drover White found himself locked out of his house, he climbed a ladder and beat the slates off his roof, believing his wife to be entertaining another man; 'That should bring them out', he said.

It was hardly surprising that after a hard day's work, drunk with power, caked with dung and numb from sheer physical exertion, the drovers quenched their thirst with frothing ale. They tottered home if they were able, or sank to the ground if they were not.

'Pudden' White was a tall man with staying power; he could take anybody on but one day he was floored by his missus when he returned, unable to fetch the supper beer from the 'jug and bottle'. Mrs White chased him from the house and knocked him out with a pudding basin full of beef dripping. Thereafter he was known as Pudden White.

Rev William McCarthy looked the man he was, every inch the cleric in a long black cassock with a leather belt encircling a waist of sturdy proportions. A breezy look about him and a ready twinkle in his eye indicated a sense of humour never far away. His facial features were strong, so was his belief that a man who was down should be helped up. He had the physical strength to go with that belief when he came across cattle drover Tubby Reed, lying drunk in the gutter after pay-off one Market Day. Tubby was hoisted to his feet and propelled home to Tucker's Row, off Newtown Road. His wife, though grateful, was doubtful whether she could get Tubby upstairs to bed, so the Vicar half carried him to the room, where Tubby collapsed on the bed in a semi-stupor. Mr McCarthy decided that having got him so far, the decent thing to do was to put the drover to bed but, glancing at the bespattered trousers and drover's boots, he felt it necessary to take off his coat, before undressing the man. He was about to fold it over the back of a chair when Tubby opened an eye. No one had ever taken a coat off in his presence unless it meant a fight, so up he got and punched the Vicar on the chin. Rev William McCarthy, ex-Navy cruiser weight, soon gave as good as he got and Tubby was knocked out cold. He was then undressed and put to bed.

In the morning, after hearing an account of the night before, his admiration knew no bounds. He had had a scrap with a real boxer, and he was full of praise for Mr McCarthy. There is no evidence, however, that Tubby attended church but he did enjoy many a free drink on repeating the story. And the Vicar? The memory of the episode never failed to make him laugh.

Teddy Joslin was employed by the Sworder family as odd job man, gardener and coachman. He lived in retirement in the coach house in part of what was formerly The Catherine Wheel in Basbow Lane where Sparrow's delivery horse was stabled. Teddy had a vegetable garden in the Lucerne Field (now the car park) where old Ben Baker grew a fine crop of pumpkins. Teddy Joslin envied Ben Baker, who was still working, looking after Tommy the horse delivering goods for the shop round the countryside, while he, Teddy, had his memories and time on his hands to watch the sun circle round St Michael's spire. To young Georgie Prior, the old coachman was a man of wide knowledge and strange behests: 'Always watch the bumble bees on the runner beans, my boy,' he would say; 'Their heads are too big to get the honey out of the flowers so they make little holes underneath. The flowers wither and drop off, and there are no runner beans' he warned.

Mrs Brace kept a small shop in High Street where she sold

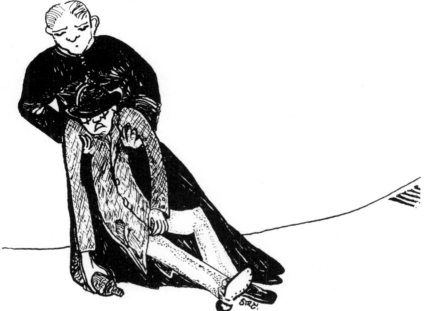

candles, bootlaces, sweets and general stores, to tide the family over the hard winter months, when there was little work for her husband, a painter and decorator. They had a neighbour, Mrs Patmore, whose house looked onto Basbow Lane. She would send young Gladys Brace to fetch her pork bellies from Olney's the pork butchers, in Castle Street, a shop renowned for its brawns and hams, puddings and pig's trotters. The savoury smells from Olneys pervaded the area. Mrs Patmore washed the pork bellies under the common pump in Basbow Lane and cooked them with the potatoes it was believed she stored under her bed. It was not unusual for neighbours to hear the potatoes rolling about on the bare wooden floor when Mrs Patmore turned over in bed.

Basbow Lane had its own fine smells and flavours. In the early 1900s cottagers took their turkeys, geese and chickens to be roasted in the bakery ovens there, when John Long took over Mrs Clarke's old bakery. The smell of hot cross buns on Good Friday was mouth-watering.

In the early '20s there was much excitement on Friday afternoons when the Misses Bawtrees, who kept an employment agency for domestic servants in what is now part of Tissimans, would hand out free religious pamphlets to the children. Books were scarce and costly and there was no free public library so the pamphlets were especially welcome. On Sundays, dressed in black from head to foot, the Misses Bawtrees would stand up of one accord and sweep out of St Michael's Church if they disapproved of the sermon.

In the small courtyard behind the shops in High Street lived Mr and Mrs Warren, pedlars. They entered the yard through a

gateway in the wall of the Boar's Head, traces of which can still be seen. Little is known about the pedlars, but when Mr Warren died in 1925, he left George Brace a gold half sovereign which is treasured in the family to this day.

'Cheer'o' Sanders, a tall breezy fishmonger, clad in striped apron, stood behind a wet fish stall near the old pump in North Street on Thursdays and transferred to Market Square on Saturdays, next to Mr Marsom from Hallingbury, who made peppermint sweets by gas flare.

You could tell that summer had come when Cheer'o Sanders changed his bowler hat for a straw boater. Mr Sanders was also a general dealer in poultry and rabbits and used to hire the White Horse Yard in North Street, where the rabbit market was then held on Thursdays, and let off parking spaces for tubs, traps and carts. There was also good stabling. Another place offering stabling was the Star Inn and a notice to that effect was still readable on the outside wall in Water Lane until quite recently.

In the 1920s, Mr Sanders' son, Tom went to work, aged 14 years, as a waiter between the bar of the Chequers Hotel and the 'commercial room'. He was responsible for the orders and found himself £1 in pocket on the first day, a testimony to the potency of the beer which farmers consumed in large quantities to wash down the jugged hare, roast beef and pheasant, offered in season on market day. Young Tom Sanders worked seven days a week for Joe Brazier, and as a treat he was allowed to go to the sea on the Hotel charabanc outings from the Chequer's yard.

Joe Brazier kept cows at South Mill Farm, where he employed two or three gardeners to produce fresh flowers, and crisp fresh vegetables for the Hotel dining room. 'Cutmore' he would shout to his gardener, 'cut more flowers!' Milk surplus to hotel requirements was sold in the town.

Charles Clarke and his son Tom were in 'horses' until the motor car and the bicycle took over. Both were employed at The Chequers, first with Mrs Chapman and then Joe Brazier. The Hotel horses were much in demand by the mail service, for funerals and for fire service and station hire and other uses in the 1880s where it would not be economic to keep a stable. Old Charles was often soaked to the skin, his fingers frozen to the reins on the occasions when he drove the big covered brougham 'taking people from Bishop's Stortford to the Asylum at

Brentwood'. It was a whole day's journey, with a short stop to rest and water the horses. He also drove The Chequers' 'brake. A fire within four miles of the town meant getting up steam before the horse drawn engine went out; beyond that a stop would be made halfway and the engine refuelled. Charles did relief driving for the mail cart to Dunmow in the 1880s. The mail left the Post Office, run by Mrs E. Millard, in Bridge Street (later Spearman & Tucker) at 5.15 pm to return to Bishop's Stortford in the small hours. One night, near the top of Parsonage Lane, a man stepped out of the shadows and grasped the reins; Charles Clarke had a long whip which he cracked, catching the man's cheek and the would-be highway robber went howling off into the darkness. One 31 January 1880, Mr Clarke was thrown from the mail cart on Hockerill Bridge when a wheel fell off; he was not seriously injured and the horse returned to Bridge Street, where it was held. Mrs E. Millard finally moved to Devoils Lane and ran the Post Office by the steps, retiring in 1897. Most at risk were the postmen—Mr W. Frear was bitten by a spaniel in Hockerill Street and was taken to have the wound cauterised by Mr Speechley, the chemist in North Street.

At The Chequers' stables, Charles Clarke gave good advice—'Always pair an old horse with a young 'un for good cornering'. It was particularly important advice when two or more horses pulled the great glass hearse.

It is anybody's guess why Fred Gull was called 'Jack Matar'. He lived by his wits and slept in the harness room of The Chequers curled up on the carriage rugs for warmth when not chased away by the then licensee, Mrs Chapman. His job was to clean the stables, brush the plumes and polish the glass hearse. There were always horses to hold on Market Day and he drove a cab to the station, for which old horses were used at six pence a cab to or from the top of Hadham Road. Once Jack Matar sat in his box all day in the hot sun; he fell asleep and was jarred awake by the slamming of his cab door—'There you are, Jack, off you go to Hadham Road' said a voice. Jack Matar set off at a good trot but when he pulled up at Maple Avenue, there was silence: 'Aren't you getting out then?' he bawled back, but there was no one in the cab. He got no pay from licensee Mrs Chapman, who had seen him drive by The Chequers' Yard and thought he had robbed her of her dues. No fare indeed. It was a nasty trick of which Jack Matar suspected Daniel Sanders, from whom he had filched a sandwich board site. Daniel Sanders was the bona fide

'Boardie', who was the bearer of anything from news about the latest production at the Great Hall, to messages urging people to prepare to meet their doom. Daniel Sanders was also a good wood chopper. 'The two never "hit it"' as Tom Clark would tell you—there were clashes of sandwich boards and insults. As horses went out of fashion, the two 'Boardies' divided up North Street and looked after cars while their owners dined at The George and The Chequers.

Tom Clarke started work at 14 years with Spearmans, the 'cycle shop. The Misses Spearman caused a sensation by being

the first ladies to wear 'cycling bloomers in Bishop's Stortford. Tom's ambition was to ride a trade 'cycle, the latest convenience. When Muffetts, the fishmongers in Potter Street ordered one late on Wednesday for delivery early next morning, being Thursday Market Day, young Tom rode to Spearmans of Dunmow to fetch it. Returning on the heavy machine, he pushed his own alongside, remembering Miss Spearman's warning just in time—'Never ride down Start Hill'. He received a jar of lemonade and a lump of cake from Miss Spearman and ninepence for the afternoon's work.

On Saturdays, the Market kept open until 9 pm so that those who depended upon the weekly wage could do their weekend shopping.

The Anchor Yard was a haven for characters—'the little man who did a good job'. There was Sam Bull, a naval type, who engraved dog's collars and cut keys and acted as a steward at the Working Men's Club, keeping a vigilant eye on the Great Hall nearby.

Mr Foreman's house boat was moored alongside. His family ran a cricket bat factory, since destroyed by fire, attached to the house known as 'Woodlands' in Parsonage Lane. Mr Foreman earned his living cutting willows along the River Stort. The fine old house made way for new development.

Car sprayer Dench operated with a builder's hand-barrow which he trailed round the town. Boats could be hired in Anchor Wharf for sixpence per hour.

A newcomer was the 'evacuee' cork factory from the Minories, Dock Street, London. The business was started by a Mr Briggs; top-hatted, he stayed active and died aged 101 years. He was joined by his son, Mr T.D. Briggs, who lived in Portland Road, Bishop's Stortford and became the oldest 'corky' in the business; he was also the longest holder of a season ticket, commuting to

110

London for 42 years. Mr Briggs imported bales of cork, which he selected in person every four or five years on a visit to Spain. The cork was 'grilled' over a fire of cork shavings before being cut up. He had the honour of supplying the smallest cork ever made, for Queen Mary's doll's house at Windsor, where the family treasures a miniature corked bottle. The firm found its way to Anchor Wharf when Mr Briggs got tired of being blown into bales of cork during the blitz. He evacuated his workers and their families to Bishop's Stortford, installing a cork cutting machine

at his home for the family to operate to speed up production. His son, Tommy Briggs, who died recently aged 92 years, was a maintenance engineer on steam ploughs and, in his prime, a well known figure in Bishop's Stortford Scouting circles. Between them these three members of the Briggs family have lived 283 years, 183 of them in Bishop's Stortford.

While some served the public, riding on pony carts, coaches, barges or charabancs, others spent years on their feet. If a man walked 100 paces from North Street to Sparrow's old carpenter's shop in Basbow Lane daily at 33 inches to a pace, multiplied by 55 years of service, this totalled 2,000 miles walked by someone like George Clarke. George walked to and from various stores and workshops several times a day in pursuit of customers' interests.

Like George Clarke, the ghostly 'grey lady' has a reputation for walking. After her busy rounds of The Causeway, she was encountered more than once by Jack Tissiman in his tailor's shop in High Street. Perhaps she it was on the way to the old Lucerne Field in Basbow Lane, where she appeared to a gardener as a grey mass. On another occasion, the grey figure was sighted in the gloomy passageway to the old kitchen of 17 North Street, then a store room, in the oldest part of the shop. A tall mass, it moved fairly quickly and was mistaken, because of its height and shape, for assistant Reuben Sapsford, but upon following Reuben into the store 'he' was seen to disappear into the back wall.

The grey lady had nothing on George Clarke, however, when it came to walking. Come to think of it, George also wore a grey coat!

The Home Guard in World War II

OPPOSITE ABOVE: North Street c1841 when Thos Bradfield was postmaster (to 1848), CENTRE: in 1909 and BELOW: in the same period on Market Day.

113

LEFT: Ben Baker, home for the night, and RIGHT: Clarke's shop on Windhill 1870s. BELOW: Teddy Joslin drinks a toast to Ben Baker's pumpkins.

114

ABOVE: Good stabling was available in the White Horse
yard in 1912. BELOW: Mind and spirit were better satisfied
at the High School and St Michael's.

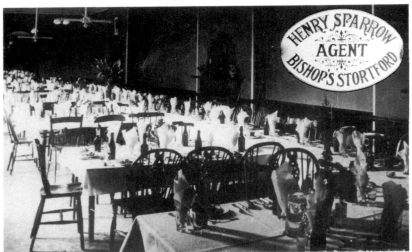

ABOVE: *The Chequers outside and* CENTRE: *in the upper dining room.* INSET: *Sparrow's name plate.* BELOW: *A 1911 badge found in a West Country antique shop.*

ABOVE: Buckler's engraving of the Black Lion, Bridge Street c1830. BELOW: All set for an occasion at the Great Hall.

ABOVE: South Street in 1906 with the Working Men's Club behind the Great Hall on the left. BELOW: Market Square c1905.

118

ABOVE: The 19th century 'steamer' fire engine. BELOW: The 1935 fire at All Saints', Hockerill.

All Saints' after the fire – in total ruin.

NEW TOWN FAIR

William Hart was born (1850) in the Catherine Wheel Alley, which was mainly inhabited by bargees, on the banks of the Stort in lower South Street. The declining barge trade forced the Hart family to find new work.

In 1895, William and his wife became the licensees of The Royal Oak, Apton Road, a situation the family was to hold for over three quarters of a century. William and his wife, a gregarious couple, organised the New Town Fair, a purely social event, with competitions like 'the lady who could drink the hottest cup of tea', a greasy pole erected on the forecourt, a tug-of-war for the men, fancy dress and 'gurling', a sport which required a number of decorated horse's collars with which the ladies crowned their faces—the prize went not to the prettiest collar, but the ugliest grimace.

One regular at The Royal Oak, Georgie Moore used to leave his donkey, 'Lolly', on the forecourt while he sampled the Benskin brew and played a game of dominoes. Miss Emma Filby would feed Lolly with stale bread. Children coming from the Filby sweet shop knew that Lolly was liable to stick his head through the hedge at the rustle of a sweet bag and gobble the lot.

Georgie Moore was as cunning as he was nice according to his mood. His Lolly always wore a straw hat, his ears sticking out through holes, and was a noisy animal who brayed in his field on the site of Vicarage Close. Donkey and master peddled fresh rabbits, skinned in a jiffy on the kitchen tables of the town, along with herbs, fruits and vegetables and George was said to be a fair man, though he got rough after a few ales. It took five strong policemen to hold him down: a small man, that was either a compliment to Georgie or the ale. He was expelled more than once from The Royal Oak for using bad language, by forceful pressure to the rear, delivered after a warning in a surprise movement by licensee James Hart. Eventually, he was tamed by a short spell in a Cambridge gaol.

121

Within the dark recesses of the Filby shop sat old Mrs Filby with her dog and pet parrot, smoking a clay pipe. A dark mysterious woman said to be a gypsy, she made 'penny surprise packets' for the children, containing a few sweets and a trinket.

Georgie's Lolly lived in Holy Trinity Parish, and he became friendly with a St Michael's dog, Rev William McCarthy's Kerry Blue, called Mike. One memorable Rogation Sunday, when members of three parishes solemnly processed down Apton Road, the hymn singing was ably accompanied by Georgie's donkey with loud and prolonged braying and Mike with excited barking.

On VE day, Georgie and his wife, who lived in Oak Street attended the street party with Lolly as the guest of honour.

Mrs Francis has good reason to remember Georgie Moore's donkey. Her father, George Coxall, grew up in New Town. In winter he earned the occasional half-gold sovereign selling crumpets from door to door. Later he became a lamp lighter for the Gas Works.

One evening, as he picked his way in the growing dusk from lamp to lamp under the dark trees in Apton Road, a white horse, which shared the Vicarage field with the donkey thrust its head through the hedge—George Coxall could feel its warm breath on his neck. He had hardly got over the shock when the donkey raised his head and brayed into his ear, an unnerving experience—he didn't stop running until he reached the Cemetery. The lamps were lit in quick succession that evening.

Mrs Francis and her husband were licensees at The Castle for 29 years. She recalls her school days 65 years ago with pleasure and contentment: climbing into scrubbed out coal-carts for outings into the countryside, singing hymns in the little shed on the Quaker Burial Ground in New Town Road. These sessions were arranged by Joseph Dorrington Day, when the money collected paid for a day's outing by train to the sea in summer time.

Cox's Farm, Great Havers sold skimmed milk at three-half-pence a pint which made good rice puddings. Hodges' Bakery offered stale huffers, twice baked in their brick oven to a crisp triangular rusk at a half-penny each; these were good value and satisfying to ever-hungry school children. There was the Soup Kitchen at St Michael's School, where children left pint and quart jugs, to be filled with thick pea soup containing pieces of chunky meat, to take home for dinner at one penny a pint and two pence per quart for large families. The boys soon composed a rude verse to describe it.

At the age of 14 years, Mrs Francis started work in The Chequers Hotel with Mr and Mrs Brazier in the '20s. On pay day she would curtsy to Mrs Brazier and receive £1 13s 4d for a month. It was a good family hotel, much used by the parents of boys boarding at Bishop's Stortford College. Boys taken out for the day could help themselves from large salvers of eggs and bacon on the sideboard. The farmers' luncheon buffet was a

feast—for half-a-crown tossed into a box, they could have as much as they liked.

The roads in Bishop's Stortford were mostly cobbled then and it was not unusual for a doctor to order that straw be strewn on the road to muffle the sound of cartwheels for those who lay sick or dying. Such a patient was Mr T. Powell, fishmonger, of South Street.

A famous corner of Bishop's Stortford, Perry's Lodging House, otherwise known as the 'old pan and can' was a row of cottages and communal room behind Perry's hat shop in South Street. One of many characters who lived there was tinker Dawney Gray, who mended pots and pans and was a china riveter. He treasured a row of small tools and drills. In the '20s, Georgie Prior took china to be mended there when he was an errand boy at Christy's shop in Bridge Street. Dodger had a special liking for live hedgehogs; prepared and covered with clay, he baked them in the embers of his fire. Sometimes he shaved off the spines; singed and cleaned, and marinated in salt water, they were ready for the stewpot, or were roasted on the end of a toasting fork. Hedgehog dripping was believed to be good for curing earache and deafness if applied day and night for two days.

Another regular, Bobby Coxall was a good-tempered man with one leg shorter than the other. New Towners called him 'Step and fetch it' as he hobbled to The Bridge public house for a drink. Despite his crippled condition Bobby entertained neighbours by dancing in New Town Road. Once a dog joined in, tripping him up to the hilarity of the onlookers. Always good humoured, he took the incident in his somewhat unsteady stride.

Permanent inmates of the Lodging House were expected to provide their own pan and can for frying and brewing up but there was always 'a penny cup of tea' to be had in the communal room where itinerants found a bed for the night. The Saracen's Head, next-door-but-one had 'penny on the liners' as well as regulars. One such regular was a well spoken quiet man, said to be 'educated' and treated with some awe on that account. He sharpened 'cut throat' razors for Christy's.

Those who could not afford a bed for the night, might 'hang on the line' for a penny. The Saracen's Head had a poor standing in local estimation. It was rumoured that there were lady-hangers-on, though they were not exactly 'penny on the liners'.

Not far away in Upper South Street, stood the Great Hall, almost opposite 'The Dells'; well named, it served the great occasions in the life of the town from the 1880s right into the 1930s—private balls and fairs, a canteen for the soldiers in World War I, musical events with the Carl Rose Opera Company, local operatic performances, midget circuses with ponies on the stage, trade exhibitions, travelling theatre companies, band concerts and, in the '20s, lectures at fortnightly intervals on a variety of subjects, including the wonders of science. On one occasion in the early 1900s, the gas was turned down and a little tube of radium was passed round, described as resembling 'moving custard'.

The Firemen's Ball and the Bachelors' Ball were occasions when Lock's dress shop and drapery, later known as Scarffs, cleared the windows for special displays of evening gowns, wraps and accessories in the 1900-1910 period. The winter season had begun. Staff usually lived in with a housekeeper to look after them. In the early '20s a mannequin used to parade in Potter Street and South Street showing off fine clothes. South Street became known as 'the monkey walk'.

Young Laurie Mitchell, apprenticed to McKensie, wigmaker to the theatrical and livery trade, was later to open a salon in Church Street. 'Aunt' Cissy Ayley acted as model for his styling and hair-dos for the big balls, in the Edwardian period, all done

with curling tongs. Most of the distinguished heads in Bishop's Stortford visited Laurie Mitchell at one time or other. Brendan Bracken, later Sir Brendan Bracken, when he was a master at the Bishop's Stortford College in the '20s, received priority over the small boys waiting for a 'short back and sides'. Laurie Mitchell excelled at the Eton Crop and the Shingle and 'coiffeurs des dames'. Only *The Tatler*, *The Sphere* and the *Illustrated London News* were allowed to litter his Salon. Latterly he was to leave Church Street when his old house made way for the extensions to Boots Chemists, and go into semi-retirement in Basbow Lane, retaining a few favoured clients who sat at the little boudoir mirror and dressing table, set with ebony backed brushes, mirrors and manicure implements, and curtains giving sufficient

125

'discreet' shade from the western sun, the window boxes lending colour and fragrance.

Like the Great Hall, Laurie Mitchell has gone. The iron gates to the old Hall now grace Monk's Walk in Half Acres—but the memories have not faded.

So too the image of Emma Dup persists; she was not the kind of lady you would be likely to forget. No-one knows why the Popes were called the 'Dup Popes'. Emma first lived in South

Street in a small cottage in a yard behind South Lawn Cafe, where Firmins, the rope and sack factory carried on business in the '20s. It was actually known as 'Pleasant Row' but was nicknamed 'The Vatican' because various Popes lived there. Emma was unique in her way. She always wore a man's cap firmly secured by a large hat-pin, her thin hair twisted into a small bun, and she smoked a clay pipe. On her feet were men's boots, a little too big; her braided dress of grey gaberdine was of uncertain age but enduring quality and was partly hidden by a sack apron; a man's jacket completed the outfit. She gathered watercress from the river which she sold from a red spotted handkerchief. She declared that her cupboard was never empty because 'the heads of too many Pope children were always in it'.

Emma invented the first shopping trolley in Bishop's Stortford, a four wheeled cart on tiny wheels which she dragged behind her, trundling potatoes from door to door; she talked to herself in a deep hoarse voice and sang her wares out in a crackling monotone: 'Buy my loverely pedatoes, bake 'em with pepper and salt and salt 'em with butter, loverely,' and when you had paid for the potatoes, she would thank you and bless you and say 'An' I allus prays to Gawd' and go on her way, a racking cough shaking her frail shoulders.

The annual appearance of Father Christmas was a familiar and welcome figure clad in red advertising the Bon Marche in South Street. There was no equal to the Bon Marche. The bill for your goods, together with the money, was propelled in a canister on an aerial railway to the elevated cashier's desk, and back came the change.

One Christmas, an assistant, traditionally dressed, was drawn round the town on a sledge, with a sack full of small items to throw to the children. Behind him, the sledge was loaded with all sorts of large toys intended to advertise to parents the wide choice available at the Bon Marche. All at once the crowd got out of control, falling upon the larger toys loaded up behind.

They took everything, snatching toys from one another. The man escaped uninjured, but it was one advertisement that misfired.

As winter approached in the early 1920s the first blast of icy wind brought a tall imposing stranger with a black pointed beard into town. On his head he wore a small round padded black cap; ringing a large brass bell, he approached South Street from the Station. No one knew who he was. He carried muffins and crumpets on a large tray covered with green baize balanced on his head. It was exciting to buy Thursday crumpets from such

a mysterious man. Occasionally he appeared on Sunday afternoons in New Town, but there was much disapproval of this form of Sunday trading.

It was in winter time too that, when the Stort was in spate at Southmill, it was apt to carry a duck or two, and the household belongings with it, through the cottages called Duck's Row and into a ditch across the road. The cottages were known as 'The Bug Hutches' and were let at one shilling and six pence per week by Joe Brazier. Lime washing the cottages was called Bug Blinding by an old washerwoman who lived there.

It was an old inhabited site near the junction with the old Stortford Road (Southmill) opposite the old Bull's Head, which may have been the site of Maple Cross. It was usual to hold executions at 'cross' roads and victims were often buried near such crosses as being a semi-hallowed place, a merciful alternative for felons and suicides barred from consecrated ground. In 1923 a curious find was reported in the *Herts & Essex Observer*. A singularly large coffin six feet two inches long, roughly hewn and in good condition was unearthed in a former garden running down to the river; the remains were of a black skull with some teeth missing, various small bones and a leather belt, but no torso. Declining an inquest, Dr Collins, the Coroner, offered the explanation that the site was a favourite spot with gypsies 100 years before. Local people were convinced that it was the remains of a highwayman summarily executed on the spot

and not unlikely that dogs had made away with the torso. The mystery remains. Whose loving care provided the strong coffin?

One morning a runaway lorry careered into the corner of Duck's Row nearest The Tanners Arms and the occupants were saved by a ton of potatoes stored under the window in the front room. The Row was then demolished (1930s).

The tow path leading from Duck's Row to the Southmill Lock cottage was a favourite walk for courting couples. Lock-keeper Alfred Chapman, a former Pearly from Hammersmith, one of two survivors of eleven brothers killed in the 1914 War, lived in the lock cottage. His job was to trim the river verges which often resulted in an unscheduled bath; he also whitened the steps and lock edges. On stormy nights, a coat thrown over his night attire, he lifted the slakers to let the water through. It often meant a walk in the dark along the river bank to Twyford to adjust the flow. Barges loaded with timber destined for Hughes Timber Yard on 'Goosemead', Bishop's Stortford required two horses for towing, and these were kept in a nearby field. One horse called Nobby objected to being disturbed once his working day was over, and courting couples were chased by him from the field which thereafter became known as 'Nobby Land'. The lock cottage is now the home of the Canoe Club.

On the other side of Pig Lane by Thorley Wash, there used to be a quaint wooden structure across the river called the Roly Croke. It was little more than a tree trunk with cantilever sides and it rolled ominously when, single file, courting couples made their way across the Stort. Mr Parsons' retriever, whose chicken-chasing habits in Sworder's field were restrained by a Thorley dog handler who tied a dead chicken around his neck till neither handler nor dog could stand it, was made to retrieve large planks of wood used in the repair of the Roly Croke. He was finally returned to his home, No 52 Portland Road, a reformed dog. The River Board has replaced the quaint old structure now by a new, more permanent one, but it lacks the old world charm of its predecessor, like so many modern changes.

Yesterday's Stortford, like the Roly Croke, is now a memory, but what a rich store that memory holds.

ABOVE: Outside the Royal Oak, Apton Road during New Town Fair, c1880.
BELOW: Georgie Moore and his Jonkey Lolly on VE Day in Oak Street.

ABOVE: VE Day at the Wheatsheaf; CENTRE: at the Castle, Newtown.
BELOW: Sidney Terrace 'welcome home' party for ex-PoW John Brace.

131

OPPOSITE ABOVE: Gas Works outing with Chafe Hutchings, Mr Stalley, Reg Baker and friends and CENTRE: Mr Player takes the Sisterhood on an outing; both '20s. BELOW: Stortford Councillors (l to r) Francis, Harry Cox, Joe Brazier, guide, Murray-Sueter MP, Harry Clayden, touring Westminster. ABOVE LEFT: Muffin man, photographed by F. Walter Taylor in March 1922. RIGHT: Jim and Mrs Holland with the then new Morris ambulance. BELOW: The Stort in spate – recently.

*ABOVE: Lock's (later Scarff's) staff and friends, c1900.
LEFT: Duck's Row in flood. RIGHT: The Old Stortford
Road, Southmill.*

*ABOVE: Wet Swan Wharf was opposite the Swan Inn
and BELOW: Duck's Row in the dry.*

ABOVE: Twyford Lock today and BELOW: the new Roly Croke.

BIBLIOGRAPHY

Bishop's Stortford, A Short History: Bishop's Stortford & District Local History Society.
Bishop's Stortford Almanac 1873–4
Bishop's Stortford and its Story: Annie Berlyn
Bishop's Stortford, The Book of: Ian Orton.
Bishop's Stortford; Accounts of: Joseph Tucker 1850
Bishop's Stortford; Postal History: Peter Forrestier-Smith
Canals of England: T. Bryce, R. Russel.
Congregational Church, Water Lane, Bishop's Stortford 1662–1962 M. G. Lewis.
Cecil Rhodes: J. G. Lockhart
Collection of Press Cuttings: Douglas Lacy.
Encyclopaedia of London.
Early Diaries 1896–1910: Hockerill Training College.
Folklore in Hertfordshire: W. B. Gerish.
Folklore in Hertfordshire: Doris Jones Baker.
Famous Authors in Hertfordshire: Rudolph Robert.
Guide to the Countryside: D. Shirley.
Historical Antiquities of Hertfordshire, The: Sir Henry de Chauncy.
History of Hertfordshire: Salmon.
History of Hertfordshire: Cussans.
The Hockerill Highway: F. H. Maud.
Herts & Essex Observer.
Into their Courts: J. G. Smith.
Kelly's Directories.
Medieval London Suburbs: K. G. T. O. Donnel.
Nonconformity in Hertfordshire: Urwick.
Records of St Michael's Church: J. L. Glasscock.
St Michael's Vestry Minutes.
St Michael's Church: Rev W. McCarthy.
Story of St Joseph's: J. Sparrow.

Figures in *Italics* refer to
illustrations

INDEX

Adderley, Thomas 39
Amateur Operatic Society ... 24
Anchor Yard, the........... 109
Anchor Wharf 110,111
Angus, John 26
Apton Road Car Park 44
Ashwell, family 40
Ashwell, James Amos 72
    Arthur 72
    Frederick............... 72,81
    Percy *38*,40,81
    Thomas *38*
Ayley, Cecil ('Doc') 52
    Cissy 125
Aylmer, Bishop........... 25,26
Bachelor's Ball 124
Bacon, Herbert 73,74
Baker family *70*
Baker, Ben............. 104,*114*
    Charlie *19*
    Reg..................... *132*
Band, the 91
Barnard, Miss 43,44
    William 43,44
    Sir Edmund 50
Barker, John 91
Barrett, Alfred Slaps 42,*45*,91,*96*
    Elsie 42
    Eva 42,73
    Ted 42,*45*
    Una 42
Bawtrees, Misses 106
Bedlars Green Brickfield 73
Beeson, Miss 48
Big Hutches, The 128
Birchanger Woods 82
Bishop's Stortford Hospital .. *14*
Blake, Hilda Jean 60
    John 60,61,62,74
Blakies Cakies 61
Blythwood Lodge 28
Boardman's *88*
Bonmarche 127
Bonner, Bishop 25
Bourne, Francis (later
    Cardinal) 51
Bowling Club............... 42
Brace, George 106
    Gladys 105
    John *131*
    Mrs 105
Bracken, Brendan (later
    Sir) 125
Bradfield, Thomas *113*
Brazier, Joe 28,*32,33,37*,94,
          100,107,126,128,*132*
    Mrs 123
    Room 28
Breweries, Baileys 40,72
    Benskins 40,121
    Hawkes 40

Briggs, Mr 110,111
    T.D...................... 110
    Tommy 111
Bryant, John 72
Buchmannhoff, Vera 24
Bug Blinding 128
Bull, Sam 109
Cage Bird Society 40
Canal 39,129
Cannon Family.............. 73
Cannon, Eliza 73
    Frederick................. 73
    Susan 73
Cannon and Son, F. 72,92
Canoe Cottage 130
Castle Cottage.............. *29*
Carver, Mr 74,*79*
Catherine Wheel, The 104
Causeway, The........... 25,26
Cemetery 73
Cemetery Lodge........... *69,71*
Chantry Gate................ *23*
Chantry, The........ 51,55,76,*80*
Chapman, Alfred........... 129
    Frank 84
    George Frederick 84
    Mrs 107,108
Christy's 124
Church Manor 60,72
Churches & Chapels, All
    Saint's, Hockerill .. 26,71,74,
                    79,119,120
    Congregational *45,63*
    Holy Trinity 49,122
    Monastery 26,52,60,83
    Salvation Army 44
    St Michael's . 43,47,58,59,71,
                    72,91,105,106
    St Joseph's 47,51,59,*64*,
                        65,71
    'Tin Tabernacle'....... 51,*64*
Clarke's 106,*114*
Clarke, Charles...... 93,107,108
    George 111,112
    Mr 58
    William *90*
    Tom 107,109
Claughton, Bishop 47
Clavering *37*
Claydon, Harry *132*
College Field 94
Collins, Dr................. 94
Congregational Tennis Club. 41
Cooper, Egbert 56,*100*
Cooper, J................... 73
Copley, H. & Co *18*
Convent, The............... 71
Corn Exchange 40,54,71
Cornwell, Tom 82

Coronations 92,*95,99,101*
Cox, Harry 28,*32,132*
    Mrs *46*
Coxall, Bobby 124
    Geroge 122
Council Office 93
Cricks Green 40
Crick, Alice *77*
    Francis 72,*77*
Crisp, Joseph ('Jesus') 40,41
Cutmore, Mr *86,97*
Cycling Club *17,18*
Day, Daisy 75,*79,80*
    Joseph Dorrington .. 41,74,75,
                    79,92,122
Death, Sarah 52,53,54,55,*66*
    Woodham................ 53
Defoe, Daniel 25
Dells, The 124
Dench 110
Denley, John 25
Dick, Miss *62*
Dockray, Dr *31*
Dodd's 74
Drinkwater, N. *100*
Duchesne, Mr 58
East Herts & West Essex News . 20
Easton Lodge............... 93
Eaton, Miss Molly ('Pussy') . 48
Ecclestone 73
Edward VII .... *93,95, et seq*
Elliott, Jock 74
Elliott Ltd, J.A. 74,*77*
Elmhurst Lodge 47
Elsenham Hall 27,*31*,93
Farms, Castle 84
    Claypits 92
    Cox's 81,122
    Exnalls 83
    Lordship *38*,40
    Much Hadham 40
    Park 40
    Piggotts 40
    South Mill 107
    Stortford Park 72,83
    Upwicke *89*
Fassnidge, Mr *32*
Featherby, George 55
    Harry George 57,75
Featherby's Works 55
Fehrenbach, Mr 51
Filby, Miss Emma 121
Finchams, Benjamin 26
Fire Brigade 59
Fire Engine *119*
Fireman's Ball 124
Firlands House 56
Firmin girls 82
Firmins 126
Flint, G. *66*
    Rene 52,53,54
    Stephen George .. 52,54,55,56
Flower Show 49
Flynn, Frank *32*

138

Foreman, family 110
  Mr 110
Fountain the (Hockerill) 87
Francis, Mrs 122,123,*132*
Frere, Beryl 56
  Laurie 56,62,91
  Phyllis 56
  Ursula 56
  W. 108
Friend, Mrs *31*
  Phyllis *31*
Furneux Pelham 84
Gabb family 26
Gammie, Dr 83
Gas Works 122,*132*
Gee, William *32*
George V 94,*99,100*
  VI *101*
George Stables, The 93
German PoW camp 42
Gilbey family 94,*100*
  Sir Walter 22,27,*31*,49,74,
                           92,93
  Tresham 56
Gillett family 81
Glasscock, J.L. 91
Glasscocks 61
Goosemead 130
Golf Club 85
Grange, The 54
Gray, Dawney 123
Great Hadham 40
Great Hall 51,109,110,*117*,
                    118,124,126
Great Hallingbury 71
Great Havers 28,81
'Grey Lady' 112
Grove Hill (now Kirby
  cottage) 28
Gull, Fred ('Jack Matar') ... 108
Hadham Place 60
Hales, Mr 83
Hall, Goldie 81
Hallingbury 58,106
Hallingbury Place 94
Harmes, family 26
  Gladys 26
  Muriel 26
Hart family 121
  James 59,121
  William 121
Harvey family 73
  Jack 73
  Toby 73
Hatfield Heath 76
Hawkes family 26
Haymeads 26,27,*31*,40,*101*
Herts & Essex Observer 73
Highland House 73
Hill, Miss Kathleen 58,59,60,69
Hockerill *31,63*
  Bowling Club 21
  Bridge 108
  Fields 82

Hodges Bakery 122
Hodson, Dr Charles 51
Holland and Barrett (now
  Budgens) 42
Holland, Grace Calvert ... *29,30*
  Jim 27,*31,133*
  Mrs *142*
Houblin, Col 91
  Estate 73
Hugh Villas 53
Hughes, Granny 58
  Timber yard 130
Humphries, Mr *32*
Hutchins, 'Chafe' *132*
Infirmary (old) 26
Inns, public houses,
  Black Bull 92
  Black Lion *117*
  Bricklayers' Arms 83
  Bridge *124*
  Bull's Head 128
  Castle 122,*131*
  Cherry Tree 26,*29*
  Chequers ... 28,*33*,93,107,108,
                      109,*116*
  Crown Inn 25,39
  George *36*,54,93,109
  George & Reindeer 25
  Half Moon 74
  Jolly Brewers 82
  Nag's Head 27,*29*,30
  Plume of Feathers 95
  Royal Oak 28,59,121,*130*
  Saracen's Head 124
  Shades 56
  Star 28,106
  Tanners' Arms 129
  Wagon & Horses 84
  Wheatsheaf *131*
  White Horse *115*
Iron Age 74
Irving, Dr 74
Jackson, George (later
  Duckett) 39,40
Jarrow marchers 26
Joscelyne's 92,*95*
Joslin, Teddy 104,*114*
Jubilees 91,92
King's Cottages 53,94
King's Head Medallion 94
Kirby, John RA Kinnersley . 28,
                             32
Lacy family 58
Langham family ....'....... 60
Larman, Leslie 27
Lilley, Puper 71
Little Hadham 81
Local Board 40
Local History Museum *69*
Lock's 124,*134*
'Lolly' 121,*130*
Long, John 106
Lucerne field (now car
  park) 104,112

Lyle family 60
Maple Cross 128
Mardon's 48,54
Margaret, HRH Princess 94,*101*
Market Day 108,109
Marshall-Taylor, Mrs 91
Marsom, Mr 106
Mason, (Cllr) Mrs G. *102*
Match Factory 42
Maxwell, A. *4,11,23*
McCarthy, Rev William . 26,48,
          54,*67*,104,122
Meads, the *23,82,86*
Menet, Georgina 94
Millard, Mrs E. 108
Millar's Works 61,75
Mills, family 74
  George 74,76
Mitchell, Laurie 125,126
Moat Farm murder *35,37*
Moore, Georgie 121,*130*
Moore, Henry *37*
Morley, Henry Percival ... 85,*87*
Morris, Dr 54,81
  Hilda 54,*67*
Mound, the (Castle Fields) .. *63*
Much Hadham 83
Muffetts 109
Muffin Man *142*
Muncer, Arthur 56
New Town 51,71,72,73,82,
                    122,128
New Town Fair 121,*130*
Newey, Nig *24*
Newey's Laundry 49
Nobby Land 130
Nockolds, Alfred 81
Nook, the 28
Norman House 47
North Lodge 53
Oak Hall 42,56,57,58,*68*
Old Hall Green 50
Olney's 105
O'Reilly, Dr 51
Palmer, Capt 93
Parsons, Archie 82
  Miss *14,55*
  Mr 130
Patmore, Mrs 105
Pawle, Capt Jack 28,*32*
Pearce House (formerly
  Plaw Hatch) *31*
Peck, Billy 49
  Margaret 50
  Sarah Anne 49,50
Pepper, Bandsman 91
Perry's Lodging House . 123,124
  Hat Shop 123
Phené Neal, Sir William 48
  Lady 48
Piggotts Manor *38*
Piper, Mr *32*
Plantation House *29*
Plaw Hatch 27,*31*,82

Player, Mr *132*
Pope & Chapman 84
Pope, Mr 84
   Emma Dup 126,127
Porter, Billy 49
   Mrs 49
Post office (later Spearman
   & Tucker) 108
Pot lids *78*
Pound, Thomas 25
Powell's...................... *64*
Powell, Mr T. 123
Prior, George 105
Pritchett family.............. 56
   G.E. 56,*68,69,*71
   Miss 58
   Mrs 58
Pryer, Amos *80*
Pye, Miss Ursula 58
Quaker Burial Ground 122
Read, Tubby 55,104
Revivalist Meetngs 27
Reynolds, Rev John 26
Rhodes, Dr W.F.R. *38,*43,44
   Cecil 43,44
Riley, Father 83,*87*
Rivers, Lee 39
Stort, ... *3,*39,47,49,56,110,
                121,128,*133*
   Thames 39
Robinson, Daniel 74
Rolf, Avery G. 41
Rolfe, Mr *32*
   Percy *35*
Roly Croke 130,*136*
Rose, Mr 60
Routledge, Mr *32*
Royal Scots *70*
Royal Staffs Yeomanry 55
Rye Street Hospital ...58,94,*100*
St Osyth's Well 25
Sanders, 'Cheer'o'.......... 106
   Daniel................ 108,109
   Tom..................... 107
Sapsford, John 51
   Reuben 112
Scarffs 124,*134*
Schools & Colleges,
   Bishop's Stortford College 54,
          83,123,125
   Convent 50
   Grammar 43
   Grimwade House *14*
   Herts & Essex High *14*
   High *115*
   Hockerill College ... 41,54,58,
         91,94,*95,101*
   Girls' 53
   National 12
   Northgate 53
   St Mary's Convent for girls *46*
   St Joseph's 92,94
   St Michael's *13,15,115,*122

Wood's, Rev John
   (British) *68*
Scott, Gerald 81
Scouts 81
Scraggs, Mr *86*
Sell, Jimmy 28
Sharpe, Dr.................... 83
Silverleys 91
Sisters of St Mary of Namur . 51
Sisterhood, the *132*
Slater's Messrs (Tayloring) .. 57
Soup Kitchen 122
South Lodge 52,*66*
South Lawn Café 126
Southmill *38,*128,*134*
Souttar, Sir Henry 85
   S. Murray *132*
Sparrow, Alice 26
   Harry *66*
   H.G. *18*
Sparrow, H. Ltd.............. *70*
Sparrow's...............111,*116*
Spearman, Misses 109
Spearman's 109
Speechley & Milbank 71,*76*
Speechley, Mr 108
Stalley, Mr *132*
Start Hill Brickworks 73
Station, the 81
Station Bridge *3*
Streets & Roads
   Apton Road... 44,81,103,121,
             122,*130*
   Barretts Down Road 81
   Basbow Lane 48,104,105,106,
            111,112
   Bell's Hill 41,*46,*51
   Bridge Street 28,*30,*55,108,
           117,124
   Castle Street 82,105
   Catherine Wheel Alley ... 121
   Causeway, the .. 25,26,*29,*112
   Chantry Road 42,56,57
   Church Street 26,125
   Cricketfield Lane *21*
   Dane Street *38,*72,92
   Deovil's Lane 108
   Duck's Row *38,*128,129,
           134,135
   Dunmow Road 40,49,73
   Elm Road 56
   Fair Green 50
   Goosemead 25
   Grange Road 51,61
   Great Hadham Road 55,
         84,92
   Green Lane (Cricketfield
     Lane) 50
   Hadham Road.........*80,*108
   Half Acres 56,126
   Haymeads Lane 27,84
   Heath Row 84
   High Street 55,*67,*106,112

Hockerill Street .. *17,*26,42,72,
        84,9*2,*108
King's Street 82
London Road 55,75
Maltings 84
Maple Avenue 74,108
Market Street 40,43,*98*
   Square ... 59,71,92,106,118
Maze Green Road 58
Monk's Walk 58,126
New Path 49
New Town Road ..49,74,104,
        122,124
North Street *11,*25,28,39,
   48,56,*70,*71,72,73,*77,*91,92,
   93,*98,*103,106,108,109,
            111,*113*
Northgate End 54,55
Oak Street 22,*130*
Old Stortford Road *134*
Parsonage Lane..... 82,83,84,
        108,110
Pig Lane 130
Portland Road .... ⁻ 55,*64,*82,
        110,130
Potter Street ... *11,*51,109,125
Pleasant Road 56
   Row, (The Vatican) ...126
Rye Street...............54,81
Sally Death's Passage ... 83
Sandle Road 28
Sidney Terrace 73,*131*
South Road 43,52,55,82,
        83,94
South Street...*17,*48,51,73,74,
   84,92,94,*96,*103,*118,*121,123
        125 et seq
Stanstead Road............ 57
Start Hill.................. 109
Station Road............52,74
Stortford Road............. 128
Thorley Hill 60,74,83
Trinity Street 82
Tucker's Row 104
Upper South Street 124
Vicarage Close 121
Vyse Court 60
Warwick Road..........49,50
Water Lane 52,106
Windhill 48,51,54,57,58,
      60,*67,*71,92,*95,*114
Sullivans 61
Swann-Powell, Sarah Anne .. 48
Sworder family 104
   Herbert 91
Sworder's *88*
Sworders field *19,*130
   market 103
Synagogue 40
Talmadge, Algernon *66*
Taylor family 26
Tee, Mr...................... *100*
Temperance Movement...40,41

140

Charabanc outing 42
Thickings family 82
George 82
'Jubber' 83
Thorley 47
Thorley fields................ 87
Thorley Lodge 52,55
Thornfields 58
Thurgood, Barry (Drover) .. 103
Tin Can 42
Tissiman 59
Tissiman, Jack 112
Town Band 42,45
Town twinning 102
Tuck, Raphael 28
Tucker, Albert 59
Joseph..................... 44
Twyford 129
Twyford house 56,62,68, 91,94
Lock...................... 136
UDC 60,92

Vander-Meulen family 94
Admiral 94
Vassall-Phillips........... 51,65
Victory Cup 19
Vineyards 40
Vulliamy 71
Warren, Mr & Mrs 106
Warwick, Countess of 93
Wesley, John 26
Westminster Bank 93
Wet Swan Wharf 135
Wharf House 56
Whiffin, Bertie 28
Jack (drover).............. 103
Mary Alice (neé Hart)..... 28
White (drover) 103
Alice 51
Mrs Ann (neé Fitzgerald) 56,104
White Horse Yard.......... 106
Whitehall.................... 58
Whittington, Alice Maria . 47,48

Dick 47
Windhill Lodge 46,51
Williams, Major.............. 92
Willetts field................. 84
Willow Springs 58
Winstanley, Henry 25
'Poor Robin' 25
Wood, John (Pastor) 53,54
Kathleen 54
Norah 54
Woodford, C.J. 28,33
Woodlands 110
Working Men's Club....110,118
Worsfold, W. Basil, MA 36
Xavier, Brother 51,52,64
Yardley, James 72
York, Duchess of (HM Queen Mother)............:.. 94,100
York, Mr 58

Index to Sketches

The Wayfarers' Rest 27
Ale for the working man...................41
Rev John Wood and his Great Dane...................53
Mr Pritchett out for a run 57
The Misses Pritchett return...................59
Kathleen Hill drives hard...................61
The 'Snobs' of Hadham Road 75
Gerald Scott lays a trail...................83
Do you like kissing old Jubber Thickings?...................85
A right Royal flap...................93
A Reverend helping hand 105
A bird for the Bakery oven 106
The Misses Bawtree show disapproval...................107
Battling 'Boardies'...................109
Mr Briggs gets corked in the blitz...................110
George Clarke flees the 'grey lady'...................111
Georgie Coxall's alarming experience 123
Emma Dup Pope's cupboard-full...................125
'Loverely Pedatoes'...................126
An expensive advertisement...................127
Mash and grab...................128
Nobby land...................129
Mr Pritchett takes it steady...................144

SUBSCRIBERS

Presentation copies

1   **Bishop's Stortford Town Council**
2   **East Herts District Council**
3   **Hertfordshire County Council**
4   **Bishop's Stortford Library**
5   **Betty Paterson DBE JP DL**

6	Violet Sparrow	60	The Fathers & Brothers, St Joseph's Monastery	108	Mrs P. Gerrard
7	Clive & Carolyn Birch			109	Mrs E. Digby Searing
8	Miss Moira Lynn	61	J.C. King	110	Mrs M.S. Brown
9	M.J.Y. Dansey	62	P.L.H. Richard	111	Mrs C. Eyre
10	Mrs M. Karolczak	63	Mr & Mrs R.D. Ives	112	Mrs E. Podgorski
11	Mr & Mrs F. Alby	64	C.J. Ives	113	Mr & Mrs A.S. Wright
12	T. Sanders	65	J.D. Piper	114	Mrs C.A. Croot
13	K. Sparrow	66	B.F. Clark	115	P. Ruffles
14	B. Willis	67	Mrs V. Briggs	116	Mrs E.M. Elliot
15	E. Davies	68		117	B. Sheridan
16	G. Markwell	69	Mr & Mrs G. Sparrow	118	T.R. McArdle
17	A. Small	70		119	Mrs J. Rushforth
18		71	S. Fuller	120	C.R. Bucel
19	B. Willis	72	Mr & Mrs D.G. Lacy	121	C.G. Clark
23		73	Mr & Mrs S.W. Brigden	122	
24	P.H. Ashwell	74	Father J. Hanton, St Joseph's Monastery	123	Mrs M.A. Whiffen
25	R.L. Ashwell			124	G. Barker
26	C.F. Ashwell	75	Mrs B. Warren-Ackland	125	Mrs M.A. Whiffen
27	C. Elliott	76	F.G. Chapman	126	B. Franklin
29		77	Miss R.S. Loadman	127	Mrs M.E.G. Turner
30	Miss C. Elliott	78	T.C. & K.A. Moore	128	Mrs R.S. Fenwick
31	Miss V. Combastel	79	Mullucks & Co	129	Mrs J.K.M. Walters
32	B. Baumgartl	80	Mrs N.M. Reeve	130	Mr & Mrs J.A.H. Smith
33	J.A. Elliott Ltd	81	Mr & Mrs Gaythorn Cookson	131	C.J.N. Lindsey
34				132	N. Tucker
35	J.A. Elliott	82	Mary & Theresa Cannon	133	E.W. Tucker
36	P. Chard	83	Mr & Mrs A. Moylan	134	Mrs F.K. Lee
37	Miss D.M. Wacey	84	Mrs E.A. Tavener	135	Mrs A.F. Precey
38	M. Read	85	Miss M. Sparrow	136	M.S.H. White
39	Victoria & Albert Museum	86	Sister Mary Martin	137	Mr & Mrs W. George
40	M. Warren	87	N.L. Fish	138	A.B. Moylan
41	V.M. Wylie	88	Mrs D. Thompson	139	
42	Miss J.M. Papworth	89	Mrs J. Goddard	140	Mrs E. Charvet JP
43		90	Lt Col J.A. Fielder	141	Mr & Mrs J. Harris
44	Miss M. Devlin	91	E. Oliver	142	G. Scott
46	Mrs D.E. Knight	92	Mr & Mrs C. Gerrard	143	Mr & Mrs H. Davidson
46	S.R. Howard Smith	93	Mrs G.I. Reed	144	L. Baxter
47	P.K. Fuller	94	Mrs I.M. Wakley	145	J.A. Brown
48	Mr & Mrs H.C. Kimber	95	Miss D. Gerrard	146	Mrs R.E. Precey
49	J.H. Lungley	96	Miss M. Gerrard	147	Mrs R. Alby
50	B.W. Ray	97	P.R. McArdle	148	Mrs M. Smith
51	Miss B.A. Goats	98	A.C. Wilson	149	F.J. Frost
52	Dame P. Friend	99	R.H. Read	150	J. & L. Boruch
53	J.K. Tee	100	J.W. Turner	151	Mrs S. Collins
54	Mrs S. Hurst-Greaves	101	R.H. Read	152	B.D. Motiwala
55	Mrs M. Whistler	102	Mr & Mrs R.F. Ashwell	153	Mr & Mrs F. Strevens
56	Mrs E.M. Butcher	103	N. Muncer	154	J.W. Golborn
57	Mr & Mrs L. Brown	104	R. Price	155	Rev. D. Jackson
58	L.C. Connell	105	E.J.C. Bromfield	156	A.N. Bullough
59	J. Rainford	106	R.W. Harrison	157	P. Forrestier-Smith
		107	D. Smith	158	Mr & Mrs G. Clarke

159 A.N. Westwood
160 Mrs D. Hutchin
161 Mrs B. Crooks
162 Mrs D.V.M. Smith
163 Mr & Mrs M.J. Richards
164 Mr & Mrs M. Roberts
165 Mrs M.E. Birkett
166 S. Gilman
167 Mr & Mrs J. Savill
168 D.W. Smith
169 D. McCarthy
170 J.R. Warren
171 Mrs R. Wilkinson
172 Mrs J.A. Alves
173 Mrs A. Greenwood
174 Mrs J.A. Osborne
175 Mrs D. Hutchin
176 Mrs L.M. Smith
177 Mrs P.J. Hutchinson
178 H.J. Barker
179 Mrs J. Player
180 Miss D. Baker
181 Mrs B. Jones
182 Mr & Mrs C.V. Mifsud
183 Miss H. Price
184 Mr & Mrs P. Tubb
185 P.H. Stevens
186 A.C. Hutchinson
187 Dr C. Bailey
188 P.P. Hermitage
189 Miss S. Fenwick
190 G. Parkinson
191 Mr & Mrs P. Dedman
192 Miss R.G. Kimber
193 Mrs S.J. Scutcher
194 D.E. Pearce
195 J. Essex
196 B.W.A. Bayford
197 Mrs Quaresima
198 J. Allen
199 Miss S. Stockman
200 Lt Col & Mrs M.A.
      Toomey
201 Mrs M.R. Fitt
202 Mrs A.L. Rutherford
203 Miss J. Hammersley
204 E.W. Bayford
205 J.C. Wetherall
206 V.W. Endridge
207 Mrs A.V. Hodgin
208 J. Sparrow
209 H.J. Monk
210 Mrs H.M. Woolley
211 Miss A. Duchesne
212 A.M. Clarke
213 Mrs M. Craig
214 Mr & Mrs A. Rayner
215 Mrs M. Gunn
216 Mrs D. Smith
217 M.J. Banks
218 E. Stanwell Smith
219 Mr & Mrs K.S.D. Hall
220 E. Simonsohn

221 St Joseph's RC JMI
      School
222 Miss W. M. Ward
223 Miss A. Alder
224 Miss M. Beatty
225 Mr & Mrs F.J. Snowden
226 Col D. Raschen
227 J.R. Whalley
228 Miss N. Ayley
229 Mrs P. Mackirdy
230 Mrs C.M. Heyhoe
231 Mrs M.E. Davis
232 Mrs J. Howe
233 Mrs J. Elliott
234 Miss E. Ashpole
235 F. Groom
236
237 M.E. Veale
238 Mrs J.L. Clayden
239 F.J. Freegard
240 Mrs H. Todd
241 A.N. Peachey
242 P.F.J. Jennings
243 J.T. Symonds
244 A.A. Ranger
245 C. Gold
246 H.J. Walters
247 C. Currie
248 P. Sparrow
249 Mrs J. M. Hollidge
250 R.B. Keatley
251 Mrs M. Pickford
252 B. Thorpe
253 Mrs A. Cove
254 J.G. Smith
255 Mrs M. Nott
256 J.D. Taylor
257 Mrs A. Holmes
258 Mr & Mrs K.H. Childs
259 D.H. Minto
260 D. Bailes
261 M.C. Offer
262 Father B.J. Crowe
263 Mrs D. Shepherd
264 R.G. Fearn
265 Miss L. Lloyd Taylor
266 J.J.F. Balkwill
267 M.R. Garguilo
268 K.M. Gribble
269 Mrs R. Morris
270 J.Y. Murdoch
271 Mrs P. Rumble
272 D. Mickelborough
273 Miss A. Bishop
274 C. Turney
275 Mrs F. Heaton
276 Miss V. Cracknell
277 E.E. Fuller
278 R. Haynes
279
280 J. White
281 Mrs Podgorski - Jarvis
282 P.S. Podgorski

283 R. Bury
284 Mrs S. Wood
285 Mrs J. Coulson
286 Mrs M. Grater
287
288 Mrs G.L.C. Castaing-
      Jones
289 Mrs M. Wade
290 Miss M. Stokely
291 Miss B.E. Turner
292 Mrs P.L. Wright
293 Professor & Mrs H.L.F.
      Currey
294 N.J. Belcher
295 Mrs J. Bradford
296 V.M. Ashwell
297 Miss S. Bradford
298 W.E. Cornell
299 Mrs K. Robinson
300 Dr & Mrs J.T. Wallace
301 Mr & Mrs M. Rhodes
302 Mrs S. Franklin
303 Mr & Mrs G.W. Searing
304 Mrs S. Franklin
305 Mrs E.E.M. Payne
306 Mrs I. Trigg
307 Mr & Mrs G.W. Buttery
308 Mrs A. Jones
309 Mrs M.A. Davies
310 Mrs A. Rand
311 Mrs I. Dixon
312 A. Jackson
313 E.M. Wedgwood
314 Miss F.M. McArdle
315 Miss C.A. McArdle
316 C.A. McArdle
317 Mr & Mrs E. McAleer
318 Mrs E. Escott
319 Mrs R.E. Lewis
320 Mr & Mrs H.G. Skerritt
321 Mrs W.G. Phillips
322 Major M.F. Osborne
323 Mr & Mrs E.A. Marlow
324 P.J.N. Clayton
325 D.K.A. Peachey
326 Mr & Mrs L.T.B. Kealey
327 Mrs Greaves
328 G.H.B. Sell
329 Mr & Mrs J.H. Gladwin
330 V.C. Wallis
331 Mrs A.E. Farrow
332 Mrs D.G. Stew
333 Mrs P.A. Ross
334 Mrs J. Platten
335 Bishop's Stortford College
336 Miss H. Powell
337 Miss A. Bradley
338 M. Tunks
339 T. Wall
340 K.S. Mollison
341 J. Burrows
342 R.C.P. Earthrowl
343 I. Greenfield

344	M.R. Devereux	364	D.L. McCormick	385	Miss B. Vermillio
345	Mrs G.R. Watts	365	Miss D.J. Drage	386	L.S. Wells
346		366	A. Beveridge	387	Mr & Mrs D.L. Hoy
347	Miss J.A. Cannon	367	Mrs J. Hodgson	388	Mrs S. Brewster
348	Mr & Mrs M.L. Woods	368	A.B. Jackson	389	Mrs K.C. Dryhurst
349	A. Bayford	369		390	D. Franklin
350	J.F. Munns	370	R.J. Dickman	391	G.H. Cox
351	Miss P. Shillito	371	All Saints' JMI School,	392	R.G. Adnitt
352	S. Bromhall		Bishop's Stortford	393	B.C. Marshall
353	Mrs O.H. Foster	372	Mrs J. Green	394	Mrs D.M. Brazier
354	D.E. Brinkworth	373	L.C. Wilson	395	Mrs B. Slee
355	Mrs B. White	374	A.G. Hodson	396	Mr & Mrs A.R. Walmsley
356	L. Flood	375	Mrs E.M. Zelley	397	R.M.R. Wood
357	E. Warwick	376	Mrs V. Walker	398	Mr & Mrs T. Wellings
358	M. Dickey	379		399	Mr & Mrs Munford
359	L.F. Martin	380	Waterside School,	400	Mrs D. Sparrow
360	R.R. White	381	Bishop's Stortford	401	Hertfordshire Library
361	R.G. Piggin	382	Mrs P.M. Lenthall	412	Service
362	Miss J.A. Sharp	383	P.G. King		
363	Mr & Mrs P.J. Chick	384	T. Green		*Remaining names unlisted*

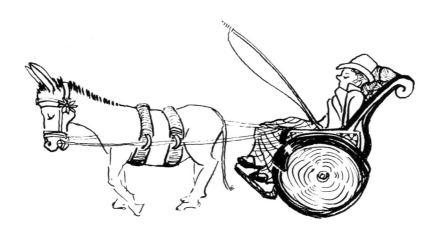

*ENDPAPERS: Bishop's Stortford from the OS map, 1st
Edition, issued in this version by Daniel Watney & Sons and
G. E. Sworder & Sons, 1917.*

144

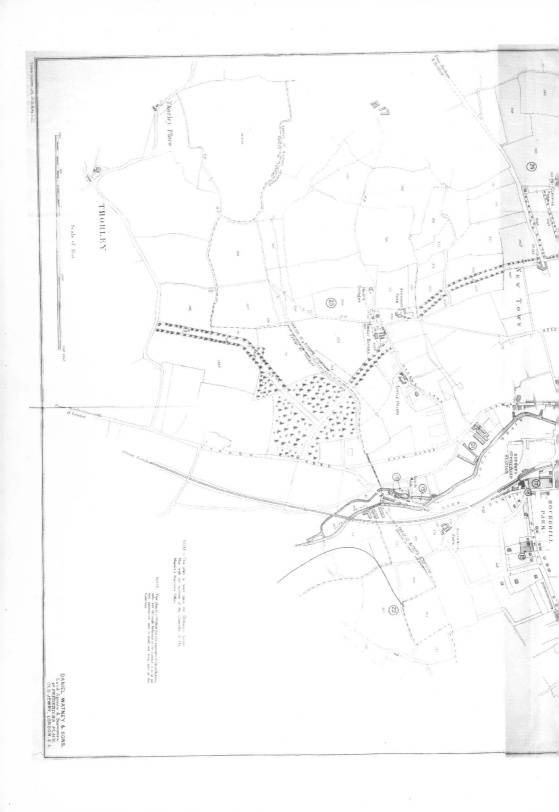

THORLEY

Scale of Feet

NOTE.—This plan is based upon the Ordnance Survey Map with the sanction of the Controller of H.M. Stationery Office.

NOTE.—This plan is published for the purposes of identification only and although believed to be correct is not so as any way guaranteed, and it shall not form part of the Contract.

DANIEL WATNEY & SONS,
Land Agents & Surveyors,
44 PRITHFIELDS PLACE,
OLD JEWRY, LONDON, E.C.